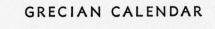

GRECIAN CALENDAR

GRECIAN
CALENDAR

CHRISTOPHER RAND

NEW YORK · OXFORD UNIVERSITY PRESS · 1962

TO MY FAMILY

ACKNOWLEDGMENTS

This whole work was undertaken by *The New Yorker* and me together, and without *The New Yorker* it could not have been done.

I have also been helped by innumerable Greek and other friends. I cannot list them all, but they know what they did for me, and I trust they know how thankful I am.

CONTENTS

GRECIAN CALENDAR

ATHENS AND VICINITY

PARNIS

Marathon

Eleusis   Kifissia   Aghios
Daphni   Andreas
AIGALEOS   Mt Pentelicon Raphina

ATHENS

Piraeus   HYMETTUS   Porto
                       Raphti

ADRIATIC
SEA

BULGARIA

YUGOSLAVIA

ALBANIA

Brindisi

ITALY

Salonika

Mt.
Athos

N

Metsovo
Corfu   Iannina   •Kalambaka
             •Trikkala

AEGEAN
SEA

Thermopylae

Ithaca   Delphi•   •Thebes

Cephalonia

Patras   Gulf of Corinth
Kyllini   Corinth   ATHENS
          Corinth Canal   Piraeus
          Mycenae   Epidaurus
Olympia   Nauplion
Tripolis• •Bassae   Sounion
Pylos   Sparta
PELOPONNESUS

MAINLAND
GREECE

ATTICA

I came back to Greece in January, 1960, with the intention
of writing about Greek "tourism," a plan that I modified as
the year went on. I came by the Greek ship *Angelica*,
sailing from Brindisi on the Italian heel. Greece is interesting
even before you get to it, because of the approach question.
There is only one Greek land frontier, on the north, and
this is cut off by the Balkan wilds from western Europe
— or simply "Europe," as many Greeks call it, in distinc-
tion to their own country, which they see as belonging to
no continent. The Balkans are an obstacle on the way to
Greece, and so is the sea. Of course one can fly to Athens,
and that is like flying anywhere else, but otherwise one
has a problem. One can take the train through Yugoslavia
— and through some gorgeous scenery — but from "Europe" that is a two-day trip. One can also drive through
Yugoslavia, but that is rough going and takes still longer.
I declined these alternatives in favor of sea travel, which I
think is the most fitting. Greece can be called amphibious.
It consists of two parts, which are sometimes referred to
as Dry Greece — the mainland — and Wet Greece — the
islands. The wet part has been moistening the national life

since before Ulysses, and if one wants to get into a Grecian mood one should (I think) get near the water.

The particular trip from Brindisi is appropriate, too, for it is small in scale, like the Greek maritime world. Brindisi itself need not detain us. In *A Farewell to Arms* one of Hemingway's Italian soldiers, named Gino, speaks slightingly of it.

" 'I am a patriot,' Gino said, 'but I cannot love Brindisi or Taranto.' "

I don't think Brindisi is that bad, though it isn't one of Italy's wonders. It is interesting historically, because even in Roman days it was a jump-off spot for Greece and Asia. It was the end of the Appian Way, and a column still stands in it to mark that fact.

As for the *Angelica*, she was built in Glasgow around 1900, and for a time was used by the Canadian Pacific Railway, under the name of *Princess Adelaide*, to run up and down the Inland Passage between Alaska and Vancouver, British Columbia. This is a common situation with Greek ships — often they have had earlier lives, in other waters, under other names. If you get up on the bridge of a Greek ship you are apt to find that the instruments have English or Scandinavian words on them. I don't think the ships have often made long voyages in those earlier lives — they are too small for that. Rather they have sailed on the Irish Sea, perhaps, or in the archipelago around Copenhagen. An impressionable tourist can get a good whiff of the Northern past, as well as the Greek present, from riding on them. I found the *Angelica* delightfully Victorian — full of old red-brown paneling and monumental plumbing. It also had two mellowing charts on display of Alaskan waters.

We embarked around dusk, then in time had dinner and went to bed, while the *Angelica* sailed out across the Adriatic. The next day at dawn we were off Corfu, a Greek island on the other coast, near Albania. I was up watching, a little after six. There were dark clouds in the distance, lit by red, and above that the sky was a pale blue, with stars in it. Corfu itself was a long, low, black silhouette, all sharply outlined, with domes and towers to point it up.

We docked and stayed there till mid-morning, and after breakfast I took a walk in the town with a fellow passenger, a young American classical scholar. "As you will remember from your Thucydides," he told me flatteringly, "Corfu, or Corcyra, helped to start the Peloponnesian War. It was a colony of Corinth, and like all Greek colonies it soon wanted to be independent. It got the help of Athens, then Corinth got the help of Sparta, and so it went. . . ."

He told me other ancient history as we walked about, and meanwhile we saw traces of the more recent past — among them massive fortifications built by the British in the nineteenth century, when they ruled Corfu awhile. The Italians have also held the place in the past, for centuries, and the culture is said to have more Italian flavor there than it has elsewhere in Greece. In ways Corfu seems almost a nation apart. In the months since then I have mulled over Greece a good deal — visualizing its map and disposition — and I find I am apt to leave Corfu out of my picture, though I have no idea if the Greeks themselves do that.

We went through Greek customs at Corfu, and for the rest of our voyage — almost twenty-four hours — we were in Greek waters, essentially. This change was more than a technicality, for we began picking up the hordes of peasants who move about on the Wet Greece shipping. The *Angel-*

ica had three classes, which is usual on such boats. The first was the only one that approached American ideas of comfort. The second had individual berths for the passengers, but these were small, hard, and crowded many to a cabin. The third had nothing but deck space and broad bunk-shelves where people could sit or lie down side by side, with their clothes on.

I have traveled in that third class on other Greek boats, and I prefer it to second for short trips; there is room to move around, along with the satisfaction of roughing it — and of course the company of Greek peasants, who are among the most gracious people on earth. From Corfu on, the *Angelica* was teeming with peasants — I was in first class, but I went down to third at times and wandered among them. They came on or got off at our ports of call. They were of both sexes and all ages, and they brought all manner of things along, including chickens, sacks, baskets, and big demijohns of wine. The chickens were cooped in crates, but their owners let them out a good deal, for water or exercise, and they scrambled on the decks along with the children.

After Corfu we sailed down the Greek west coast in fine weather, with a blue sky and blue sea. The hills ashore were sometimes gray and bare, sometimes green with a brush cover — they always looked dry in either case. We stopped briefly that afternoon, without getting off, at the islands of Ithaca and Cephalonia, the former having been the home of Ulysses. No trace of his town or palace has been found there yet, but one gets a fair notion of his environment by just gazing from the boat. Ithaca is a hard, rocky little island, with much character but little luxury — Tennyson hits it off well in his poem *Ulysses*. From a mere glance at it one sympathizes with Ulysses' expressed longing to get back to it, and also with his actual delay in doing so.

That night we turned into the Gulf of Corinth, which cuts almost across the Greek peninsula, and at dawn we reached the Corinth Canal, which finishes the cutting by a few miles of ditch across an isthmus. The Canal was dug in the nineteenth century, but the idea of it is much older than that. Even Nero set out to dig it, but he stopped before long, and I have heard a strange explanation, from a Greek tourist-guide, of why he did so — that he was dissuaded by some hangers-on, whose motives were not specified, but who convinced him that the Adriatic Sea, in the west, was higher than the Aegean, in the east, and that its waters would pour through the Canal and swamp the island of Aegina, near Athens. (I have not confirmed this story, I must say, from any other source.)

There was a faint dawn as we approached the Canal, then as we entered it this was dimmed out by electric lights along the waterside. They were like streetlights on a New York highway — the Canal was no wider than that, and for the first part the banks were low. Soon they rose up, though, and in time we were passing through a deep cut of buff stone or earth, with only a few feet of room on either side. The water of our wake rushed and splashed in the interval. Later we passed under two bridges, one for trains and one for autos, which appeared to sit up in the sky along with the stars — they were, I think, more than two hundred feet above us. Then we left the Canal, with its illumination, and the dawn showed pink and green by that time — the roosters in third class were crowing.

The Canal is a big factor in Wet Greece. Boats of much size can't get through it, so it helps to keep Aegean shipping down to the cozy Greek scale. Non-Greek shippers sometimes complain that it is discriminatory, designed to keep them out of Greek waters. It doesn't keep them out entirely — not even from the Canal itself — for I have seen Italian and Turkish boats in it. But they were small by the standards of their nations, and their captains may well have been grumbling, too, about unreasonable delays rigged against them by the Greek Canal authorities. The Canal is small, the ships are small, the Aegean is small — it is all a small world of its own. Its true capital is the Piraeus, which despite its great age and importance is also small, and frequented mainly by the toy-sized merchant marine. Athens is the official capital of Greece, but many of the island people look on it as a mere shadow of the Piraeus, although the latter, to a hasty tourist's eye, seems hardly more than a miniature Hoboken.

By the time we reached the Piraeus, an hour or two from the Canal, we had a good sunny morning. I disembarked, got into a taxi with my things, and drove up through Athens to a resort named Kifissia, in the hills beyond it. I had stayed there the summer before and had grown attached to a hotel, the Cecil, where I planned to live for the next few months, until the tourist season got under way.

The Cecil is one of the pleasantest hotels I know, in Greece or anywhere. It has been kept so largely by the conservatism, even the parsimony, of the Greek brothers who own it, and who firmly refuse to put in swimming pools, tennis courts, chromium bars, public radios, or any other gadgets, despite the example of their competitors and the world at large. What they have, as a result, is a fine, simple, old-fashioned structure whose design reminds one of a hospital and also of the Potala at Lhasa, the former center of Tibetan Buddhism. The building is a wide, shallow slab, about six stories high, rising from a verdant part of

Kifissia not far from Mount Pentelicon, where much of the marble for the Acropolis was quarried. Like many other Greek buildings, the Cecil has a good deal of marble in it, too — marble stairways, marble terraces at front and back, and marble in the bathrooms.

The hotel's layout is simple and very like a hospital's — each floor has a wide, straight corridor running through it, with rooms on either side. When I arrived, in winter, the place was nearly deserted, and only the lower part was heated. I got a room and bath on the "second" story — the third, by our reckoning — for only two dollars a day. It had a parquet floor, a high ceiling, a high, narrow, hospital-like bed, and French windows, these looking out southward — across the driveway — to a stand of evergreens, and beyond their tops to Athens and the Aegean. We often had good weather as the winter continued, and then I would open the French windows and take sun-baths. We also had snowstorms on occasion, and then big flakes would hover dreamily outside.

The staff was small in winter. On my floor there were two men-servants and a chambermaid; in the dining-room there was a headwaiter, a waiter, and a bus-boy; and in the lobby there was a concierge and two or three other porters or bell-boys. I can't describe how kind they were to me. Some Greeks say their countrymen are afflicted with *xenomania*, or madness for foreigners. I have detected no madness in it, but they have got a tremendous courtesy, cheerfulness, and sense of hospitality. A foreigner almost always gets from Greeks a smile, a pleasantry or two, and whatever help he needs. This was especially true at the Cecil, which seemed to have a very high morale, although the servants were not paid much. I went through my days continually supported by good cheer.

Soon after I arrived I began taking Greek lessons, from a lady who came in twice a week, and after that the servants all joined in to coach and give me practice. They were better linguists than I ever hope to be. Aside from Greek most of them spoke French and English at least. The head-waiter spoke English that was more than adequate for his job, though I understand it was less good than his Italian, his French, his Arabic, or his Turkish. The concierge, George, was highly voluble — touchingly so — in both French and English. He was a thin, nervous man with a long nose, bushy brows, and thinning hair that he kept smoothly brushed.

George was always solving my problems — lending me money and telling me how to get things done in Athens. He used to tell me about *his* problems, too, including his nightmares. He even had nightmares of lions coming and beating on his chest, and he sometimes inveighed to me passionately, and suddenly, about injustices in Greek society. But I think he was happy on the whole. He had good cause to be. He had married off his sisters — an onerous duty in Greece, where dowries are the rule — and was raising two fine little non-dowriable boys of his own.

For my taste the food at the Cecil was only so-so, or *etsi-ketsi* as the Greeks say. Most dishes on the menu were of a type that I associate with the word "tourism," which came, in 1960, to have a phony connotation for me — they were feeble imitations, that is, of French, British, or other West European models. The Greeks have a good cuisine of their own, but when they start turning out wiener schnitzels and tournedos rossini they achieve products not much more edible, in my opinion, then color photographs of food. Yet the idea is current that quality folk must eat such things, and if you are caught in the meshes of high-level Greek tourism you may never taste anything else. The big hotels in Athens concentrate overwhelmingly on photograph food, and so the city's cheap restaurants, as a rule, are better than its expensive ones. The only case I know where one can gain something by eating at a big Athenian hotel is in the Grande Bretagne at lunchtime, where they do roll around a fine collection of *mezedes* or Greek hors d'oeuvres. Otherwise I would recommend those hotels only for bed and breakfast.

As for the Cecil, it offered seventy or eighty per cent photographs, perhaps, but it always had a few Greek dishes too. The Greeks favor lamb or veal stewed with vegetables in olive oil, and one such stew was usually available. The Cecil was also terribly good with *moussaka*, a dish made from layers of ground meat alternated with either eggplant, zucchini, or artichoke hearts — depending on the season — then wet with olive oil, topped off with a little cheese and dough or mashed potato, and put into the oven.* In most restaurants the *moussaka* is baked in big pans, for many portions, and left standing, so it gets cool, but the Cecil always did it fresh and piping hot in individual dishes. Sometimes a dish was left in the oven too long, perhaps, but the oil always kept it juicy.

---

* It isn't really so simple, I have learned since writing the above. To make *moussaka* you slice the vegetables and fry them. You cook the ground meat in oil, with onions and other flavoring as desired. You put a layer of the vegetables in the bottom of a pan and put the meat on top of it. Meanwhile you will have made a white sauce as follows — heat butter and flour in a pan together till the flour is cooked; beat in one or two eggs; add milk gradually, to make a thick sauce; and continue cooking, adding cheese if desired. When the sauce is done, pour it over the meat in the pan, then bake the dish in an oven. The formula can be varied — the layers can be made more complex, the sauce can be mixed with the meat layer, etc. And potatoes can be used instead of the eggplant or other vegetable.

Olive oil is a great feature of Greek food — it sloshes about everywhere. The Greek oil seems to be thicker than the Italian, but also light somehow, and tasty. One gets addicted to it, to the detriment of one's figure — though one doesn't have to worry much about butter, which is scarce in Greece; the oil takes its place. It is proper in Greece to put a lot of oil on salads and then sop up the remains with coarse brown bread.

The Cecil had good salad material, but its bread was pretty photographic — no fun to sop with — and we should not pursue the salad question farther now. The Cecil is really not a good occasion, at all, for discussing Greek food. I might add, though, that every morning, in my room, I had breakfast consisting of tea, yoghurt with honey on it, and — at that season — very juicy oranges. The oranges came mainly from Corfu, from the island of Crete, and from the Peloponnesus — below the Gulf of Corinth — and they were cheap and good till well into the spring. The yoghurt was made in Kifissia, I think from sheep's milk. The honey was often labeled as coming from Mount Hymettus, east of Athens — a famous source in classical times — but I don't think much of it really did. Anyway it was good — the Greeks are honey fanciers — and on the yoghurt it was wonderful. (I say I think the yoghurt was made from sheep's milk, but there is a seasonal factor here that I haven't figured out. Ewes have lambs only at certain seasons, and therefore give milk only at certain seasons too. Cows, on the other hand, are not seasonal in this regard — or not very seasonal — and among them give milk the year round. Therefore even in good sheep country the yoghurt is often being made from cows' milk, though I have yet to check on the exact Kifissia calendar in this.)

Until Easter I kept clear of writing about Greece, not feeling ready for it, and I also did not pursue tourism diligently, as the season for that was yet to come. I secluded myself in the Cecil, went on the wagon for Lent, and practised writing of another kind. Of course I went into Athens often, and kept up my Greek lessons, and read about Greece, but I did these things in a peripheral way — I was shy of assaulting Athens too directly.

My only other activity worth talking about, at this stage, is the walking I began to do, on and near Mount Pentelicon, which takes up the ten miles between Kifissia and the sea-coast to its east. I have walked a good deal for years now. I have theories about why one should do it — that it is good for the health, is conducive to thought, makes one able to observe things at close hand, etc. — and I think all these arguments are sound, but the main point is simply that I enjoy walking; I feel calm and happy while doing it. Greece is a good country to walk in, too — it is fast being motorized, with new highways shooting out in all directions, but as of today much of its life still moves on foot, and can be reached only on foot. This is true even of Attica, the promontory surrounding Athens, and it is even more so of the lesser islands and more distant mountains. Anyone visiting Greece would do well to practise walking beforehand — it is especially desirable to get one's feet hard, as the paths are apt to be rocky.

I was not in good shape when I came to Greece this time — I had been walking but little for the past few months — and so I set about improving myself. I began walking for half days out of the Cecil — on Sunday mornings — then for whole days or close to it. The days were still short then, but I found that in six or seven hours, at my

natural slow speed, I could reach Attica's east coast, from
where I could get home by bus.

The plain and bay of Marathon, where the Persians
were stopped in 490 B.C., is over on that coast, to Pentelicon's northeast. You can't see the plain well from the
mountain's summit, because of an intervening peak, but if
you walk over the spurs in certain ways you can get good
views down onto it, and then can descend on it yourself.

Pentelicon is interesting, too. It was being quarried then as
never before, since there was a building boom in Athens. On
weekdays I used to hear drills and blasting on Pentelicon;
and great areas of the mountain's south side were white
with new heaps of marble-chips.

When walking on that part I could look down toward
the Acropolis, ten miles away, and could imagine how the
work must have gone under Pericles. At least one famous
Athenian sculptor — Phidias, I think — used to visit Pentelicon and choose his own marble from the quarries. It must
have taken him half a day to get to the mountain, I have
figured, and then I suppose he camped there for a while.
The quarried marble blocks were moved down the moun-
tainside on tracks or skids, and one can still find the marks
of such operations in the stone. There is at least one ancient
quarry on the mountain, too — a big straight cliff-like cut,
with brush growing off its top and with a grotto and other
indentations in its base, including a primitive Byzantine
chapel, which may have been preceded on that site by a
pagan shrine.

The age of such holy places is hard to learn. It is known
that there were sanctuaries on Pentelicon in classical times
— there was a huge statue of Athena there, for instance,
and caves that were sacred to Pan. Then the early Christians
used the mountain for worship, apparently hiding out

from the Romans. Under the Byzantine Empire it probably had less attention, but under the Turks it seems to have had some fugitive Christians once again. Any grotto or other sacred place there might have been used and re-used, with alterations, during all these changes, but the experts have not yet untangled the story. So one gets little precise information on Pentelicon. What one does get, in walking there, is a sense of great age, adorned with repeated quarrying, worship, and herding of sheep and goats.

The guide-books available on Greece are poor, for the most part. There was a Baedeker in the days when such books were good, but this is out of print now, and much of it is cut of date as well. The most obvious modern substitute is the *Guide Bleu*, published by Hachette in Paris, but this is sketchy on some things and so enragingly pedantic on others that many people give it up in disgust. There are other, more readable guides — such as that edited by Fodor and published also in Paris — but these, while giving interesting impressions of Greece, do not go into much local detail. This failure of guide-books seems to be a world-wide condition now, barring subsidized efforts like our own federal guide project of the 1930's, and one suspects that the times are too uncertain to justify a writer's giving such a book the long devoted care required, or a publisher's giving it the investment. So one gets hasty improvisations instead of the detailed, well-proportioned works that one would like.

As a result the best available guide to classical Greece is still the *Description of Hellas* written by Pausanias in the second century A.D., and brought up to date with a commentary by James G. Frazer, of *Golden Bough* fame, in the 1890's. Pausanias traveled through all the more celebrated parts of ancient Greece, except the islands, and wrote voluminously on them; then Frazer followed in his foot-steps and brought him up to date still more voluminously — sometimes he even took off, too, and wrote about things that Pausanias had omitted. Between them the pair have done a building-by-building — if not a stone-by-stone — job of coverage, but it comes in six chunky volumes and is also out of print. It is not a work for the casual tourist to buy, transport, and brandish among the ruins,* but it is excellent in libraries, where scholars and low-speed travelers may dip into it.

Concerning Mount Hymettus, Pausanias said that it "produces the best food for bees [in the world], except for the land of the Alazones. For the Alazones leave the bees free to follow the cattle to pasture, and do not keep them shut up in hives; so the bees work anywhere, and the product is so blent that wax and honey are inseparable."

To this rather mystifying statement Frazer later added — among other things — that the Alazones had been a Scythian tribe in South Russia; that the bees on Hymettus still had thyme, lavender, savory, and sage to eat; that their output had been praised by Horace, Ovid, Cicero, and Pliny; and that they were said to have put honey in the mouth of Plato when he was a baby.

So it went. Pausanias said that in his time there were bears and wild boars on Parnis, another mountain near Athens, to which Frazer added that there were still boars on Parnis when he checked up, and even on Pentelicon (though I got no hint of them in 1960). Pausanias men-tioned the shrines of Pan and other gods that abounded in

---

* The best book, in English, for a traveler to carry is probably *The Oxford Companion to Classical Literature*. This is an encyclopedia, not a guide-book, yet it is handy in size and contains a wealth of informa-tion on ancient Greece (as well as ancient Rome). Its scholarship is expert, its style terse and clear. It is a little gem.

the Attic landscape, and Frazer rediscovered most of these and reported on their condition. Pausanias, sticking his neck out, said of the Marathon battlefield that "here every night you may hear horses neighing and men fighting." Frazer capped this statement with a long list of other ghostly sights and sounds to be enjoyed on old battlefields, including that of Napoleon "passing like the wind" at Marengo. One feels *The Golden Bough* a good deal when reading Frazer's Pausanias. One also has a pleasant time out of it, at least if one is living on the scene.

I cared less about Attica's ruins, though, than about her landscape as a whole, and what had happened to it in ancient and modern times. Of all great states of the past, Attica is perhaps the most easily visualized by someone on the spot. This is especially true of its heart, the so-called Athenian plain. The plain's southern edge is the Aegean shore, centering on the Piraeus. Then from there it slopes gently upward for some fifteen miles, passing Athens itself rather early in the game, and ending eventually, after expanses of fields and pastures, against some mountains. The plain is, in fact, hemmed in by mountains, except for the narrow passes that open through them. There is Hymettus on the east, then Pentelicon on the northeast, then Parnis on the northwest, and finally Aigaleos, a lesser eminence, on the west. In ancient times the mountains guarded the plain, the plain grew the food, and the food nourished the city that clustered around the Acropolis — in bad times the Acropolis was a safe refuge, and in good ones the Piraeus was a fine outlet for trade. That, in essence, was the foundation of Athens's greatness — the outer parts of Attica, like Marathon beyond Pentelicon, were subordinate, and had been since the dawn of history.

I could observe the foundation as I walked around, and

meanwhile I saw the modern city planted on it. Athens is growing fast and chaotically now. It is no longer distinct from the Piraeus, though the centers of the two are five miles apart. It has spilled up against the bases of Hymettus and Pentelicon, too, and is threatening to spill against Parnis, which is farther away. It is also up against Aigaleos in the west, and in that quarter there are patches of new industry. These patches, together with the heart of Athens itself, throw up a pall of brown, dusty smog on most days, so that the visibility over the city — famous in history for its clarity — is often poor now.

(The smog doesn't reach the mountains yet, but modern times are being felt there in other ways. During 1960, even as I walked, a huge radar device was set up on top of Pentelicon. Hymettus has some vast new beacon on it, too, and Parnis has a couple of such installations plus a new hotel. Even Lycabettus, a nice little peak right in Athens, has acquired unsightly antennas recently, and it seems that the Acropolis itself is the only height still sacred.)

On my Sundays in winter it often rained or snowed, but as a rule I walked anyway. Sometimes I got wet through, but sometimes, too, the sun came out and dried me again. The herdsmen on the mountain would be out in the rain, of course — they couldn't come in. They wore big heavy woolen capes in winter, and on stormy days I would see them squatting in these for long stretches, with their backs to the wind. Their clothing seemed old-style and traditional for the most part — made of felt or homespun — but an occasional modern thing — a GI-style cap or coat, for instance — might appear in it.

On the mountain's upper slopes the herdsmen tended goats almost exclusively — the sheep of Attica, it seems,

are kept to the rich and easy lower ground. I believe that
the herding of goats on Pentelicon is illegal, actually, since
they are thought to prevent a new forest cover, which is
badly needed, from growing up there. A Greek planning
expert once expressed doubt to me that there was anything
more formidable than single tethered goats on the whole
mountain. But he was wrong, and I used to see flocks of
over a hundred there. The goats were black for the most
part, and with their horns they were apt to have a weird
look, almost like that of insects, as they nibbled at the stiff
green brush. Each big flock had two or more dogs with
it, and one or more herdsmen, the latter living right along
with the animals, sleeping with them, and sharing their
fate for the moment. The dogs were nondescript, and
smaller than Tibetan mastiffs, but still they were fierce.
They growled and barked and showed their teeth as I
passed by, and they seemed capable of hurting a defense-
less man. But stones are handy in Attica, and I used to
pick one up and show it — tossing it a little — whereupon
the dogs would slink away.

My impression was that the goatherds on Pentelicon
stayed in the open for days at a time, but they did have
bases — chiefly on the mountain's northern side, toward
the Marathon plain. The sheepfolds or goatfolds there were
of pine-boughs. They looked like extra-wide brush huts
without roofs, and in principle they resembled the traditional Mediterranean house, with a courtyard in the middle,
and with sheltered space surrounding it — the latter being,
in this case, merely a circular lean-to.

The herdsmen's houses, also of brush, but fully roofed,
were not much better than their animals'. Those goatherds
lived a very primitive life, more so than that of the farmers
in Attica, or even of the shepherds, who were closer to

the plains and the amenities. I got to know these classes superficially as the winter wore on. I could talk with them a little and ask them the way. They would answer partly by gestures. The Greeks have a wonderful method, which I have not seen elsewhere, of pointing in three dimensions. They will make their hand swoop up and down again, to indicate that you must cross a mountain at some stage. Or they will run their hand straight out, then curve it to the left or right to show a turning. It is a graphic method, hard to describe in words, but most helpful in communication; it is one tiny manifestation of what I hold to be a superiority, in many respects, of Greek culture over others.

The giving of directions was always done gladly on the mountain. I think this was partly because of the Greek nature and partly because of a camaraderie that springs up between people who are walking over the same rocks and up the same steeps. I claim that if one walks with any gusto one is respected by other walkers, and I even boast that it is a good thing, nationalistically, to have a few Americans walking about in far countries. It explodes the generalization that we have forgotten how. Again and again, while walking in Attica, I have been asked whether I was a German or an Englishman. I was neither, I have answered — certainly not; I was an American; and I have felt that some of the nonsense about our country was dispelled thereby.

There are two reasons, I think, for the rockiness of Greek paths — the country itself, which is rocky in the extreme, and the fact that hoofed animals are the paths' main users. The link between hooves and rockiness is a rule of life, apparently, and I have seen its workings elsewhere. In China, where the paths are used almost entirely by humans, they are smooth, but right next door on the

Tibetan plateau, where yaks and mules come into play,
they immediately get rough and rocky and dusty. In Attica
the rockiness often appears as a coating, on paths, of
sharp, prismatic gravel, and one must watch one's step.

Some paths are wide and much traveled, some so narrow
as to be hardly discernible. Many of them represent centuries — millennia — of thought and experience, and so far
as I have learned they always follow the best route. It is
often tempting to strike out for oneself when walking in
Greece, but if one does this one usually gets trapped in
thick brush or a dead-end ravine. So paths are important,
and the type of path is important, too. Those used by
donkeys and mules nearly always lead from one settlement
to another, while those used only by goats may lead into
wilderness. One learns to tell the two apart by the tracks
and droppings on them. One can also tell goat- from sheep-
paths by the droppings, and this is useful because of the
sheep's greater tendency to stick to civilization — a goat-
path is a snare, always being apt to peter out on a clifftop.

Attica had two false springs that winter, when the air
was sunny and balmy for days on end. Fruit trees bloomed
on the plains then, and crocuses came out all over Pentelicon. Yet these spells led only to new frosts, and the real
spring did not begin till just before Easter. Then green
leaves sprouted on the gray branches of the fig trees, and
green tendrils on the grape plants, which in the winter had
been pruned back to stumps the size of one's forearm.

I saw all this while walking, but then I interrupted the
process — I went for Holy Week to Mount Athos, up in
Greece's north, and when I came back the green had burst
out everywhere. I made a seasonal change in my work

then — I began writing articles about Greece itself — but I didn't leave the Cecil and I didn't really change my activities; I merely intensified them.

It was in May that I reached the high point, for the year, in my language study. Up through May I took lessons regularly, and did homework on them, but in June I tapered off. As a boy I had studied ancient Greek, after a fashion, but since leaving college I had forgotten most of it — and I don't know, anyway, whether ancient Greek, as taught in our classrooms, is a help or hindrance in learning the modern kind.

From it one remembers the Greek alphabet, at a minimum, but the sounds of that alphabet have changed so much that even this is of doubtful value. The hard B, G, and D of classical Greek have all gone soft in modern. The letter B — *beta* — which used to be pronounced "bee," is now pronounced "vee." This means that Βορηάς — known to us as Boreas, the north wind — is now pronounced "Voreas." It also means that a new way of writing the hard B has to be devised, for the sake of words borrowed from other languages. This is done by putting an M sound before a P; the word "bar," for instance — a dispensary of drinks — which is common in Greek, is written μπάρ, which by our schoolroom methods of transliteration would be "mpar."

In much the same way Δ — *delta* — the old D sound, has softened to a deep TH (as in "them"), and the gap has been made up by writing an N before a T; "divan" in modern Greek is ντιβάνι, which by classroom transliteration would be "ntibani."

Similarly Γ — *gamma* — the old hard G, has faded to a Y, or merely to a rustle of the soft palate, and has been replaced by a G before a K sound — "garage" is γκαράζ, or "gkaraz" as the classroom would write it.

For these reasons the signs in downtown, cosmopolitan Athens carry much bewilderment for a pure classical scholar — "Wagons-Lits Cook," for instance, is written Βαγκον-Λι Κουκ in Greek, which the scholar would tend to read as "Bagkon-Li Kouk."

That isn't the whole story, either, for many vowels and diphthongs in Greek have changed, too. Especially η, ι, υ, ει, and οι which used to be pronounced "ay," "oo," "ee," "ay," and "oy," are now all pronounced "ee." The old short and long O sounds — O and Ω — are also pronounced alike now. These consolidations puzzle not only foreign classical scholars but also the Greeks themselves, who often cannot tell by ear just what vowels they should write into a word — it is almost impossible, according to my teacher, for a Greek with anything less than a high-school education to be a good speller.*

My teacher's name was Miss Sophie or Sophia (which means wisdom). She was a young lady of radiant complexion and the purest character imaginable, who had taught herself both French and English. In the mornings she ran a nursery school and in the afternoons she gave Greek lessons to foreigners in and around Kifissia, going from one to the other, rain or shine, on a bicycle. My lessons were held at first in the Cecil's lounge and then later, when the weather got warm, on one of the marble terraces

* The Romanization of Greek names and words in this book follows no strict rule. "Γ" may be represented by "g," "gh" or "y," "δ" by "d" or "dh." An attempt is made to convey the sound if it seems important, but not in a true grammarian spirit. Often the supposed classical pronunciation of a word is followed, too, and here again the style of Romanization is variable.

outside. We studied from a grammar-book and practised conversation, telling each other about our daily doings.

I was determined to concentrate on "demotic" Greek — *dimotiki* — and Miss Sophie went along with this, though sometimes, I think, against her better judgment. Modern Greek is a hard language, and not the least of its troubles is the conflict between *dimotiki*, the common man's tongue, which is vastly corrupted from the ancient one, and *katharevusa*, a more stately medium that has been kept near the ancient by literary emulation. The clergy, the legal profession, and the bureaucracy in Greece use *katharevusa*, and thus keep it firmly entrenched, although the uneducated can't handle it and although the young intellectuals are dead against it. Respectability is on the side of *katharevusa*, youth and change on that of demotic — nearly all modern Greek fiction and poetry is in the latter. Sentimentally I would have favored demotic anyway, I suppose, but there was a practical reason in support of it, too, for I wanted my smattering of Greek for use with peasants, waiters, bus conductors and the like, rather than the educated, who I knew were often fluent in English themselves.

My study of Greek isn't worth dwelling on. I became able to order a meal with it, to exchange politenesses, or to get a hotel room. Beyond that I didn't go, and the accomplishment had little use, but it was a pleasant and interesting thing to do, and a way of learning more about the country.

In spring the vineyards grew, the days got longer, and I stretched out my walking. I took to leaving the Cecil at noon on Saturday, walking to Raphina, a little port on Attica's east coast, spending the night there, walking along the shore itself on Sunday, and coming home that evening as before. I would carry a knapsack with a change of

clothes, a bathing suit, a book, and so forth. I would walk
to Raphina by the path system in Pentelicon's southern
foothills, a nearly straight route that would take about six
hours, with a stop for lunch and perhaps a later one for
refreshments. At the start of the trip I would still be virtually in the Athenian suburbs — walking among little masonry summer-houses, like sugar-cubes, that had been built
there by the poor. After that I would be in near-wilderness
for a couple of hours. Then at the end, in descending on
the coast, I would be on roads again, and for the last half
hour would actually be on asphalt, though it would be
pleasant then — smooth and comfortable in the dusk, and
with few cars on it.

In Raphina I would go to the Hotel Diana, a simple little
place with bare rooms and white enameled bedsteads. In the
early spring I would take a hot bath there, then later — as
the evenings grew warm and light — I would take a swim
in the ocean, for Raphina has a good beach. When dressed
I would go to a fish restaurant, of which there are several
excellent ones in the port — little establishments on a street
that curves around the waterfront.

Raphina is not the best place in Attica for seafood — the
best is a small subordinate harbor in the Piraeus, called
Tourko Limano, where one may sit outdoors and eat a great
variety of fish and other things, including sea-urchins, oys-
ters, and several kinds of clams. But Raphina is probably
second to this place for variety, and it is infinitely better
than the Piraeus for walking or swimming.

I used to find many kinds of fish on sale there, plus
shrimps, lobsters, octopus, and squid. In the restaurants in
such places one is supposed to choose one's own fish from
the icebox, and Greek men are great experts at this; they tap
and feel all the fish, and gaze into their eyes, and thereby

get the very best ones, or so they believe. I am not versed
in that art, though, and I would usually just have a quick
look and point, or merely tell the proprietor my wishes.
Often I would have fried *calamarakia*, or squids, which are
a great delicacy — they might be classed, vaguely, with our
own fried scallops and fried clams, but I think they are better. Or I would have red mullet — a tender, tasty, flaky
fish — grilled over charcoal and wet with olive oil.

If I had mullet I would probably have some octopus before it. One could write a whole book about the octopus,
which is eaten in all Greek settlements near the sea. It hides
under water in the rocks, I understand, and is speared when
it comes out. It is never very big; its body is smaller than
a football, and its arms are no more than two feet long —
I don't know where the fearful giant octopus of Northern
fancy comes from. These Mediterranean octopuses are not
fearful to man, anyway, but are said to be very much so to
lobsters, which reputedly go all to pieces on seeing them.
The Greek octopuses are tough, and are beaten to make
them tender. Once in the islands, during the summer, I
watched three men hurling octopuses, rhythmically, against
a cliff for more than half an hour. Greeks also beat octopuses
with clubs, and rub them across rough stones. They cook
them in various ways, but the most common is to boil them,
let them chill, and serve them, cut up, with olive oil and
capers, as an hors d'oeuvre.

The octopus must have been a feature of civilization for
a long time — octopuses abound in Minoan and Mycenean
art of more than three thousand years ago. The octopus
makes a lovely motif because of the freedom and rhythm
in its arms — it is especially good for painting on pottery,
for an octopus can be made to cover, or embrace, a pot in
various satisfying ways. Many of the golden octopus orna-

ments found at Mycenae, oddly enough, have only seven arms, though nature and language call for eight. Whatever is the reason for this — and the experts haven't found it, to my knowledge — it seems true, anyway, that in Greek art the octopus is always a thing of pleasure and beauty.

Before or after the fish I would have a green salad — perhaps of boiled dandelion-greens or wild asparagus, perhaps a mixture of sliced tomatoes, peppers, ripe olives, and bits of *feta*, or crumbly cheese — the whole of this wet down with oil and a little vinegar and consumed with the help of bread, which in those restaurants would be the good coarse-grained stuff of the common man. If I wanted dessert I would usually have cherries at that season — delicious whether red or white.

The drink accompanying it all would be resinated wine, called *retsina*, usually white then, though pink at certain other times, and sold in carafes from casks right on the premises. *Retsina* is overwhelmingly the favorite drink of the taverns in Attica. It is cheap, being made from grapes grown near at hand, on the Attic plains, and flavored with resin from the Attic pine trees. In the foothills of Pentelicon I have often passed trees that had been tapped — a gash would have been made in them with an axe, then part of an old tin can would have been nailed on below it, to catch the gummy sap. This seems to be the universal method now — getting resin and adding it to the wine — but I have been told that in ancient times the flavor came from pine staves in the casks themselves, and that the resin was useful as a preservative. Now other preservatives are available, and there is no pine in the casks, but the people of Attica, and many other parts of Greece, have become addicted to the resin taste.

Some Americans don't like *retsina* — I know one South-

ern lady who says it tastes like North Carolina — but I have
grown fonder and fonder of it with time (I am apt, I must
confess, to let my palate be governed by my enthusiasm for
a country). Those sympathetic to *retsina* can get pleasant
side-effects by merely passing under pine trees. When on
the wagon in Lent I used to get very thirsty when smelling
pines, or even just hearing them. I like to sit among pines,
too, when drinking *retsina*, especially on a sunny, windy
day.

Arising at Raphina, I would have all of Sunday for walking on the coast, with swimming interjected now and then.
Raphina is off the southeast corner of Pentelicon. I could
walk north from there, between the mountain and the sea,
and reach the plain of Marathon, or I could walk south and
skirt another plain, called the Mesoghia — the "Center of
the Earth" — which lies below Pentelicon and east of Hymettus, and is the most fertile part of Attica. It is especially
rich in grapes, and I went through parts of it, in the spring,
where green vineyards stretched interminably on every side.

If I left the coast, on these southward forays, and circled
back through the Mesoghia, I could get home on foot by
nightfall. Otherwise I would push on downward, in the
afternoon, and turn inland eventually to catch a bus. There
were several busy market towns in the Mesoghia, and these
had good road communications, though the country around
them seemed much in its ancient state — many classical remains have been found in the Mesoghia as well as pre-
classical ones, going back to Mycenean times, which even
Pausanias didn't know about. The plain seems to be an old,
old theater of civilization — it was probably once independent of Athens, having its own relations with the Aegean
world, on which it fronts directly to the east.

If I stuck to the coast I would lunch at a *taverna*, as the

Greeks call their less pretentious restaurants — either on the
bay of Marathon, if in the north, or at a place called Porto
Raphti in the south. (This is a little harbor with a big statue,
dating from Roman times, on an island in its mouth — the
people, through the centuries, have come to liken the statue
to a tailor, or *raphtis,* so that they call the whole place
Porto Raphti, or Tailor's Port).

The *tavernas* at Marathon and Porto Raphti — small es-
tablishments, mainly outdoors — were delightful in early
spring, but as summer drew near they became crowded.
The Greeks love nature; they like nothing better than to
pass a Sunday in it; and in summer the heat of Athens gives
them an extra, violent push toward it. As a result the beaches
of Attica swarm then with holiday folk, who are much more
urban than the peasants and fishermen there already, but
still less fully in the machine-age than a crowd at, say,
Jones's Beach would be.

In regard to the machine-age, Greece is still a backward
country. She was backward in the 1930's, and the war and
civil wars of the 'forties and early 'fifties have kept her that
way. Now she is trying to catch up, and her people are
acquiring new gadgets in which they revel — and in whose
capacity for noise-making they seem to revel especially.
They honk the horns of their autos with abandon, and they
are wild about little transistor radios, which they take to
the loneliest places and turn on, listening to scratchy rendi-
tions of almost anything. These radios began appearing in
the coastal *tavernas* as spring wore on — planting themselves on tables and competing with each other — and after
that the landscape was not the same.

I got a strong warning of this change on May first, which
is the spring-festival day in Greece, and which in 1960 fell

also on a Sunday. It is a day, I have learned since then, when people hang up — on their houses — wreaths made from various plants, and when they also, customarily, swarm into the country with unusual fervor. But I was ignorant of this when I left Raphina that morning and headed northward, going toward Marathon.

The first odd-looking thing I met was a group of the local people — both grown-ups and children, all well-dressed — moving past me toward Raphina and each carrying a bundle of bright-colored toy shepherd's crooks. They meant to sell them, and I later saw others doing so, much as people sell fancy canes at our county fairs.

I passed them and kept on for two or three more miles, along a coastline not very accessible to the public, and after that I came to a resort named Aghios Andreas — Saint Andrew — which I found already crowded, at nine or ten in the morning. Holiday folk were everywhere there, on the grass and underneath the trees. The middle-aged ones were spreading provisions out, and many of the youthful ones had begun to sing and dance — boys and girls together in a circle, in the Greek fashion. Other people were wandering about, enjoying the sun, the air, and the sea. I was accosted by a pretty red-haired girl, with two little boys in tow, who said she had come from the Piraeus that morning and who asked me to sit down and join them. I did so for a while, and we had a halting conversation, after which I said good-by and continued northward.

I had to move inland for a little way, to get around an army camp, but when I had passed that I returned to the coast. I found a rock to hide behind and changed into my bathing trunks, after which I sometimes waded and sometimes walked along the shore, moving ever northward and meeting, and greeting, city folk of all descriptions.

By one o'clock I made Marathon, and the *tavernas* there were a madhouse, with autos pulling in, dust flying, children crying, radios blaring, and people squirming everywhere. I managed to find a table on the beach, though — beneath some matting in a breeze — and there I lunched eventually on octopus, grilled lamb, tomato salad, cheese, and pink *retsina*. I say "eventually" because the service was agonizingly slow that day, a condition I was to find in resort *tavernas* throughout the summer. Such places hire little extra help when summer comes, although their business increases fiftyfold. The same old servants must stagger under the new load — and I've seen them really staggering, too, especially the little bus-boys, who go around in a daze on heavy Sundays.

The weather was hot that day, and after lunch I was of two minds whether to walk home or take a bus, but I settled on walking. I struck out inland on the plain, first passing a big mound where the Greek heroes who fell at Marathon are buried, then crossing the highway, then going through some olive groves, and finally coming out in open grain fields. The fields were very green, and the sun was bright.

I was not sure of the path — I wanted to try a new way over Pentelicon's spurs — and I worked down to the plain's southern edge, where I met a shepherd. He had a few dozen sheep and was grazing them along the border of the grain fields — carefully, it seemed, to keep them out of the grain itself. I walked and talked with him awhile, telling him I wanted to go to a village called Stamata, which was *epano* — "up on top" — and I pointed. He told me I was on the right track, and I left him and pushed onward, coming in a mile to a village called Vrana. It is a poor and primitive-looking place, but is on an ancient site — a rich town of the Persian War period, according to Frazer.

In the village outskirts I met an old woman dressed in widow's black. She wanted to sell me some eggs, but I said no, thanks, I was just walking for my pleasure. Then I mentioned Stamata, and she pointed out the path to me; it went up a hill near the village and soon disappeared in a gorge there, and she informed me — roughly, by three-dimensional gestures — of its course thereafter. I started up it, and before I had climbed far I met two German boys with knapsacks coming down, who told me there was no trail ahead, only wilderness. But I kept faith in the old woman and climbed onward, passing through an empty cluster of goatfolds and then finding the trail again, after a moment of obscurity. It turned out to be a fine one, although steep and rocky. It had nicely calculated switch-backs, and its grade was never really trying. It must have been very old, I guessed — the main route between those heights and the plain — and it may have been the way actually used by Phidippides in bringing the news of Marathon to Athens. I didn't run up the hill as he did, of course, but walked slowly, stopping once to rest and read awhile.

After an hour amid wilderness the path leveled off, and then I came to a tiny cultivated field in what looked like a glacial hollow. Above and all around it were gray rocks and scrubby brush — not a sign of habitation. I went on, passing a few more fields in time and crossing a rocky barren, and soon I came out on a wonderful swale of tall, green, succulent wheat, with no less than three big flocks of sheep being maneuvered around it. The place was rich looking, but still it had no visible links with modern times or the machine-age — I had seen no machinery, indeed, since way down on the plain. After passing that spot I continued for another mile, perhaps, then climbed a hill and reached Stamata itself, which still looked, as I entered it, like a village in another age. But on its far side I found an asphalt road, with cars; and I was back in civilization.

In that fashion I passed my spring weekends. After May Day the crowds along the beaches thinned a little, but then they thickened again. As June drew near, it was plain that I must change my beat, which I was ready for anyway, as the tourist season had begun. I was due to travel.

II

THE SEASON BEGINS

I began my summer of tourism by taking a cruise on a chartered yacht with fourteen other Americans who lived in or near Athens. I shouldn't really call this "tourism," perhaps, for a stranger couldn't easily have joined in — the trip was arranged months ahead by people who knew each other and knew Greece. Yet tourists *can* take similar trips, and while on this one I ran into some cousins of mine from Chicago who were doing just that — they and another couple had flown out and were batting around the islands in a small boat that they had chartered directly from home, through a travel agency. They paid more per capita than we did, and they had less advantage — through ignorance of the language and of local ways — in the arguments that forever come up with one's captain in these cases, but otherwise it was much the same.

We paid only ten dollars apiece, each day, for everything, which I think must be the bottom price for yacht excursions in Greece — it was reached only through the most expert shopping for food by our lady shipmates.* Our boat

---

* But cruising in a *caïque* — a native island boat — can be cheaper still, especially if you do your own cooking.

was named the *Toscana;* she was eighty-five feet long; and she had normal berths for fourteen plus a sofa, or bench, on which slept the fifteenth, a pretty Greek-American girl named Penny Pappas, who in due course fell out of it, in rough weather, and got a black eye. Our guiding spirit, or commodore, was also a Greek-American, named Brian Bojonell; he was the Pan American Airways man in Athens, a born diplomat and an expert on travel — it was he who got us all together, chartered the boat, and dealt with the captain on the voyage.

We set sail from the Piraeus on a Friday evening and returned there on a Sunday nine days later, having meanwhile called at the islands of Delos, Mykonos, Icaria, Samos, Patmos, Kos, Kalymnos, Amorgos, Naxos, Syra, Kea, Aegina, and one or two others that I can't remember. The *Toscana* itself called at the Turkish coast of Asia Minor, and the passengers then aboard her went to see the ruins of Ephesus, but I was not with them, having carelessly left my passport behind. I was marooned on Samos that day along with the cook, whose papers were likewise defective, and I had a glorious time walking through the Samian landscape and viewing strictly Samian remains. In fact Samos is the first island worthy of much mention here. Delos and Mykonos are notable indeed, but I was to spend a month on the latter, with frequent trips to the former, in midsummer, and I shall postpone writing about them for later. Icaria, the third island touched, is a dull one as they go,* and it was Samos that first really caught my fancy.

The islands of the Aegean seem helter-skelter, but most of them are classified in groups. The largest group, which

---

* On our trip we saw only the south side of Icaria, which is straight and unrelieved, without even a true harbor. But travelers who know the island's north side praise it highly.

spreads right out from Attica, to the southeast, is called the
Cyclades, or "Circulars," because they are seen as lying in
a ring — "respectfully," according to a lady guide I know
— around Delos, one of their number, which is the supposed birthplace of Apollo. The Cyclades are close together,
and when among them one usually has several in view at
all times. They are the most likely first step in an Aegean
trip, and we both came and went through them. We stopped
there, it happened, but had we gone straight through, the
passage, timing it from the Piraeus, might have taken some
eighteen hours.

Then beyond the Cyclades, to their east, comes a gap
of open water, which takes several more hours to cross,
and beyond that lie the Dodecanese ("Twelve Islands"),
which are near the Turkish coast and which culminate, at
their southern end, in Rhodes. The other well-known islands in the Aegean, apart from these two groups, are usually thought of as singles: Crete below the Cyclades, Hydra
near the Peloponnesus, and Euboea, Lesbos, Samothrace,
etc. in the north.* Of the singular northern islands Samos
is the southernmost, being right above the Dodecanese and
separated from them not geographically so much as historically — the Italians held the Dodecanese, but not Samos,
for instance, between the two world wars.

Samos's own history is richer than that of many a whole
country. It was the home of Pythagoras, whom we remember mainly from geometry class, but who was also a great
international sage; he is said to have traveled for decades
in countries like Egypt and Persia, bringing home Eastern

* Actually there is a third main grouping in the Aegean — the
Northern Sporades, which lie off Euboea. (The western Greek islands
— Corfu, etc. — are not counted here, as they are not Aegean, but
Adriatic.)

lore and interpreting it for the West, together with his own ideas and discoveries, through a large school of philosophy. In his lifetime Samos also had a famous tyrant, Polycrates, who made the island a strong power, but who, according to Herodotus, was much too lucky — luck being thought dangerous in ancient Greece, as arousing the jealousy of the Gods. Amasis, the king of Egypt, advised Polycrates to break his luck by throwing away something valuable, so he threw a ring into the sea, but a few days later it turned up inside a fish he had been given. Amasis would have nothing to do with him thereafter, predicting that he would come to a bad end — and predicting rightly, for he was crucified by the Persians.

Samos has had an unusual later history, too — it was wholly depopulated under the Turks, for one thing, then repopulated with settlers from other parts of Greece. The story goes that a Turkish officer went hunting on the deserted island and was so enchanted by it that he got special authority for this repopulation from the Sultan. One can understand his enchantment, for there seems to be a spell on Samos even now — to me it repeatedly called up the fairyland touches in Shakespeare's lyrics. The Cyclades and Dodecanese are brown and bare for the most part, but Samos is green and wooded. It is also a biggish island, thirty miles long, and one end of it is a real mountain — nicely domed, laced by gorges, and supporting lonely villages on its upper slopes. One can see all this from afar, and one really looks at it, for there is no other landscape to distract the eye.

We approached Samos on a sunny afternoon, most of us being spread on the *Toscana*'s deck. The mountain was hazy blue at first, then greener; the lonely villages were all white; and we had this prospect for an hour or two. Then we

drew near the coast and began running along it, after which
our view changed, of course, and the villages above us
changed, too, appearing and disappearing in the spurs and
gorges. They could be reached only on foot or horseback,
we could see, by tiny-looking mountain trails, and though
in plain view they were the remotest-seeming things imaginable. We ran along the coast for a few hours, then at
dusk we tied up in the island's main harbor, which is called
Vathy, or "Deep" (the older part of the town — built on
a slope beyond the easy reach of pirates, who used to be
numerous in the Aegean — is called Epano Vathy, or "Upper Deep").

We all spent the next day in sightseeing and enjoying
ourselves on Samos, and I spent the day afterward too. On
a coastal plain some miles from Vathy there are ruins of
a gigantic sixth-century B.C. temple of Hera, and I went
there on both days. The temple was lovely — or its scant
remains were — but the thing that fascinated me was the
plain, which at that moment was throbbing with life and
greenery. It was big, flat, and rich. It took me a couple of
hours to cross it, and as I walked I saw people bent and
toiling in the fields almost exactly, I felt, as in the time of
Polycrates. The plain must have been a leading factor in
Samos's wealth and power then — another being the timber
on the mountain, which enabled Polycrates to build a fleet.
His capital had been on the plain's inner edge, and the Hera
sanctuary was on its outer one, near a gravel beach where
the waves pounded. Between the two had grown the grain
that had paid, one imagines, for the travels of Pythagoras
and for much of the Hera sanctuary itself, which was one
of the great works of ancient architecture.

Classical Greek civilization really began in the islands —
they flowered in the sixth century B.C., whereas Athens

flowered in the fifth — and few places, one would guess,
flowered more than that very plain.* Of course the plain
was beautiful in itself, without all this dusting off of history.
It had a complex irrigation system, which made it hard to
cross, because the canals were too wide to ford, and one
also couldn't spot them in the distance, to head around them.
One had to ask directions and plan in advance. Besides irrigation, the plain had birds and insects galore; and the grain
on it was just right for early summer, being at full height,
but not yet turning yellow — just a perfect, luscious green.
The sun was hot, too — so hot that I wore a wet towel on
my head while walking there.

Other things that I noticed especially in my two days on
Samos included the horses, the houses, and the sea-urchins.
The horses were fine and Arab-looking, walking freely with
a long stride, and I suspected that their quality was linked
with the island's nearness to the Asiatic mainland — Turkey is a little over a mile from Samos, across the channel.
The houses, too, were more in the Turkish style than in
the Greek, thanks to this same nearness, undoubtedly, and

* In this book the word "classical" refers to the Greco-Roman civilization that arose in or before the sixth century B.C. and lasted to the
fourth century A.D., when Christianity replaced its pagan faith. Yet
the word "classical" has a more limited meaning, too, that should be
noted. As used by art historians, for instance, it refers to the Greek
flowering, dominated by Athens, that began in the first half of the
fifth century (after the Persian Wars) and lasted till the late fourth,
when Alexander ushered in the "Hellenistic" age (by unifying the
Greek world and expanding it to Asia and Africa). In this narrower
sense the classical age was preceded by an "archaic" one, around the
sixth century, when Greek arts and letters were coming up fast in
the islands, thanks partly to Asiatic influences. Pythagoras and the
Samian Hera temple belong to that "archaic" period. There is a similar
narrow use of the word "classical" with Rome — referring to arts and
letters down through Augustus. But here it takes in all the ancient
high civilization of Europe except for the Minoan and Mycenean eras.

thanks also to the availability of lumber; they were mainly wooden, that is, and had shallow balconies or overhangs in their façades, whereas the houses on most Greek islands are of masonry and are more simply cubistic in design.

As for the sea-urchins, I put my hand on one when climbing out of the water at Vathy, and my fingers were sore for a month thereafter. In effect, if not biologically, a sea-urchin is like a porcupine or hedgehog. It is an assemblage of spines or quills whose points break off in one's hand or foot and fester there. Amateur surgery can't remove the points without further damage, it seems — at least that available on the *Toscana* couldn't — and my policy was to leave them alone. They hurt me for a month in a dull way — not enough, for instance, to keep me from using a typewriter — and then they dwindled and disappeared. The experience taught me to give sea-urchins a wide berth, of course, and I kept an eye out for them the rest of the summer, as they are common in Greek waters. They are blackish in color, round and spiny in form, and a few inches in diameter. They cling to submerged rocks along the coast and rarely move, so far as I know — it is hard to see how they *can* move, of their own accord. Their weapons are wholly defensive, but potent, and I don't know what animals prey on them aside from man. Even the preying by man seems rather forced — a gourmet stunt — as the edible part of an urchin, inside the shell where the spines converge, is very small.

From Samos we went south into the Dodecanese, traveling in good weather. We had had some rain at Delos and Mykonos, but that was to be the end of it — the Greek spring showers were nearly over by that time, and the Greek summer, which is dry, was on us. The *Toscana*'s sails were up, to catch a following wind, but in the main we were running on our engine, as we did throughout the voyage.

The captain was in high spirits that morning, and he moved among us on the deck, joking and showing us things through his binoculars. He was relieved that the expedition to Turkey was behind us. Greek-Turkish relations are uneasy at best, and this happened to be right after the Turkish coup d'état of May 1960, when the army there overthrew the "politicians." The day we had left the Piraeus, Turkey had sealed her borders off, and at Samos the captain had refused, on these grounds, to make the promised trip to that country at all. He had finally been overruled because the promise had been put in writing, by the chartering agent, and because we were told in Samos that all was calm again in Turkey. But he hadn't liked the idea. He had gone sadly and returned gladly, and now he was feeling fine.

He and we were having one of our rare honeymoons, indeed, but it didn't last. We were heading for Patmos in the northern Dodecanese, where Saint John the Divine wrote, or dictated, the Apocalypse. We neared that island around noon, whereupon we asked the captain to head for a certain beach, known to some of us who had visited Patmos before. When the beach came in sight he looked at it through his glasses and declared that it was of gravel, not sand, and that we should try some other place. Yet he plainly couldn't tell at that distance, so we insisted, and the beach turned out of course to be sandy, and excellent. He had wanted, I think, to go straight into the harbor of Patmos, tie up there, and let us swim off the boat or seek out a beach on foot, which would have saved him fuel and effort; and this experience was typical. He was a wily man. He had a hard life on the *Toscana*, full of worries and responsibilities — for he had come to own the boat as well as merely sailing it — and he didn't want to make things harder by catering to our whims unnecessarily. His interests were at variance from ours, in fact; there was argument much of the time; and I think this is pretty general when foreigners go cruising with Greek captains — it is as well to have much of the program laid down, in writing, ahead of time.

We passengers were disunited, too, with different tastes, and inclined to drift as the captain willed it. Some of us wanted to see antiquities. Some wanted to swim and take it easy. Some wanted to wear fine clothes and seek romance. Once ashore we were like a herd of buffalo on the plains; one of us would see a tempting item somewhere and would wander toward it, and the others would follow; then someone else would see an item in another direction, and we would wander there; and so it would go. There were a few exceptions to this aimlessness; one lady of our number, especially, was a determined sightseer, knowledgeable on ruins, and often insistent that we get our money's worth in seeing them — it was she, I believe, who really made the captain go to Turkey, for the others didn't care much.

On the whole we took things as they came, and I must say we had a good time of it. The captain lectured us once for our poor co-ordination — we were going ashore by launch at the time, very much in driblets, at a village that had no jetty. He said that being out of step that way was an American trait, and he may have been talking sense, too, for he had observed many nationalities. Just before us he had taken out some Swiss, I think, and later that summer I saw him, at Mykonos, with a load of Belgians — he had long been booked up for the season, from all directions.

He was a thin man, with a seamed and weatherbeaten face. The *Toscana* also had an engineer, short of stature and dressed usually in a beret and pea-jacket; two deck-

hands, bronzed, barefoot, and taciturn; a cook, who was
fairly nondescript; and a cabin-boy or steward, a tall, thin
youth named Antony, who did the work of two men, what
with cleaning the cabins and running food and ice for us —
he even served as a deckhand in emergencies.

In the Dodecanese we called at Patmos, Kos, and Kalymnos before turning back toward the Cyclades. At Patmos
the important spot, historically, is the grotto where Saint
John is supposed to have had his revelations, but a more
spectacular sight is a Byzantine monastery on the hill above
it. This monastery is old, dating from the eleventh century,
and has outstanding murals, treasures, and manuscripts in
it, comparable to those on Mount Athos — furthermore it
can be visited by women, as Mount Athos can't. It stands
amid a white and glistening village, on the hilltop, which
looks almost like a snowfield as one sails toward it.

Kos is a large island with many classical remains, but these
are less noteworthy, on the whole, than others elsewhere
in Greece (they are of special interest to doctors, however,
for Kos was a medical center in antiquity, with mineral
springs; a shrine to Asclepius; and many associations with
Hippocrates, who lived there — a huge, old plane tree stands
near the harbor at Kos, and it is claimed that Hippocrates
taught and practised under it).*

Kalymnos, our third Dodecanese island, is the center of
the Greek sponge trade. It is a bleak spot, with craggy
rocks going up on every side from the port — a purely
mineral environment, with as little softness to the land as
one finds in, say, Manhattan. The divers sail out of Kalymnos in the spring, going to parts of the Mediterranean or to

---

* Many fine pieces of Hellenistic sculpture have been found on Kos,
too, and some can be seen in the museum there.

the Red Sea and beyond, and they come back in the fall, spending their winter relaxing, celebrating, and working their sponges over. Their life sounds like a hard one — deep-diving off small boats working out from larger mother-ships, the latter being scantily supplied with food and water. Sometimes a diver gets the bends, from going down or coming up too fast, and then he may be paralyzed — such cripples can be seen in Kalymnos. Sponges of every sort may be seen there, too, of course, and purchased, though the great majority are exported — England and West Germany are the best customers. The sponge trade is in decline now, because of plastic imitations. If it dies, the human life on Kalymnos will be hard pressed.*

The islands that one merely passes, in the Aegean, are nearly as interesting as those one calls at. They are of all sizes and shapes, but always brown in summer amid the blue, at least in the Dodecanese and Cyclades. Some of them are large, low, sprawled, and complex. These can be a bright sienna, say, in the foreground, then fading off to a hazy rabbit-brown in the distance. Other islands are little flat bars. Still others are shaped like turtle-shells, or like brown thimbles. Often the big ones, even, seem lonely and deserted; one sees only cliffs there, coming down to the sea. But usually there is a little white church, at least, glinting off on a peak. Sometimes there are white villages on the coastal plains, beneath the mountains. The mountains can be steep. Sometimes they have a jagged or wavy silhouette, and always they are dry-looking. Often, even if an island

---

* I bought a hat-sponge on Kalymnos, which has served me well. It is conical, and I think the organism must have grown upward from its narrow end, like the outer casing of a cauliflower. After being gathered it was later trimmed, and it fits me like a neat cap made of material an inch or so thick. I wet it and wear it when basking or working in the sun.

is lightly settled, its hills are criss-crossed with stone walls, and in the afternoon these, with their shadows, look like black strings laid on the brown. The islands seem almost beyond counting. Besides the score or so one often hears about — and the few score others that are named on the charts — there are a host of seemingly anonymous fragments, down to little barren rocks. The settled islands were much used as places of exile in Roman days, incidentally, and at least a couple are so used today — as concentration-points for Communists or those suspected of Communism.

Each important island has at least one harbor, and often this has a curved waterfront, the quay itself being faced with masonry and paved with flags. The paved area goes back some distance, making an equivalent to the *plateia*, or public square, that is thought indispensable to an inland Greek settlement. The area may be shaded here and there by plane trees, and at its inland edge there is a row, also curved, of shops and cafés, the latter having tables and chairs in front of them. Everything looks at the waterfront, along which small boats are tied up, often with their sterns to the shore — it is customary for Greek vessels to land by first dropping an anchor out in the harbor, off the bow, then spinning around with this as a pivot, and finally backing in.

The *Toscana* landed thus at many little ports — all on the toy Aegean scale — and when she was tied up we passengers fanned out on the shore to stroll, have a drink, or do some shopping. Sometimes I went to get a shave, for they are cheap in the islands — ten or fifteen cents apiece — and hot water was hard to come by on the *Toscana*. If we felt like walking we could pass through the village behind the waterfront — sometimes a distance of only a few score yards, which would put us in the outskirts.

A few ports had windmills in their outskirts, with white

cloth blades that made them look like daisies. There were always plenty of smaller real flowers in the village gardens, too — hibiscus, bougainvillea, blue morning-glories, oleanders; on Kos the oleanders grew as big as trees, and were even shaped like trees. Nearly all the islands we touched at grew figs, grapes, olives, and miscellaneous fruit trees too; some of their more sheltered spots grew oranges and pomegranates. But trees were not the islands' forte, and as we pierced into the countryside we saw little but brown grass and rocks ahead, enlivened here and there by goats or a donkey — there was scant machinery around, for the machine-age is slow in getting to the islands. If we pressed on up a hill — and there often *was* a hill behind the port — we might look off the other side to emptiness: to nothing but honey-colored slope, that is, running down to the azure sea.

On clear days, which are the rule in summer, the Aegean is always an intense blue — sometimes many shades of intense blue in a single vista, sometimes one solid shade, like the bluest of blue paint in a can. At times the water has a blinding silver sheen on it, from the sun. At others it has a lot of whitecaps, and then the blue is dark. When calm the water is surpassing clear, and if one swims on it with a snorkel-mask, near rocks, one sees jewel-colored fishes lit by the most brilliant light. If one swims at a beach one also has a sense of clarity, and I have usually opened my eyes when under water in the Aegean, though I rarely do it elsewhere in an ocean. I think (perhaps erroneously) that the Aegean is less salty than the Atlantic or Pacific — it tastes less salty, besides feeling less so to my eyes, and there is a good reason for it to be less so, too, in that it forever receives the great rivers of western Russia, which come down to it through the Black Sea, the Bosporus, and the

Dardanelles. I have swum in the Black Sea and Bosporus as well, and have found them strikingly free of salt, and I look on the Aegean water as part of that progression.

There is another progression, that of air, that affects the Aegean in the summer. This is felt on the spot as a nearly constant north wind, which I have been told comes down from the cool zones of Russia to fill a vacuum created over the Sahara by hot air rising there. Be that as it may — and the explanation sounds plausible — the north wind, called the *meltemi*, is a main fact of life on the Aegean. It blows with few interruptions, and it keeps the islands cool as well as nagging at the islanders in their pursuits. Its force varies, and the stronger gales are classified as chair or table winds, depending on which of those objects they can blow over. There is even said to be a super-gale, called a bell wind, which can ring the bells in the island churches, though these are ordinarily mounted in little tunnel-like vaults, atop the gable ends, that run from east to west, or across the *meltemi*'s direction.

On the *Toscana* we encountered what must have been a table wind when almost a week out, on a Friday. As luck would have it that was the day we crossed back from Kalymnos, in the Dodecanese, to Amorgos, in the Cyclades, a trip of some forty miles through the gap between the two groups. At first we were in the lee of Kalymnos awhile, and the waves, though big, were not extraordinary. I was sitting out on the bow, watching them, when the captain sent a deckhand out to call me back. From then on we were in the open sea. The bow was repeatedly under water; the decks were nearly everywhere awash; and we had great difficulty in moving about — merely to stand erect on the pitching deck was heavy exercise, and I was stiff from it that night. The wind kept up all day. We had a break for lunch, in the lee of a small island that showed up, and then we went out and battled through the afternoon again, making Amorgos at dusk.

While we were in motion the only sheltered spot on deck was astern and to port of the cabin and the wheelhouse, and most of us passengers who were not seasick gathered there. Even there we got salted thoroughly with spray, but it was a lovely spot to be in. The crew was busy and heroic-looking, going forward to lash things down, or merely standing alert while clinging to some support. The captain was at the wheel, dealing artistically with the big waves, one by one. The little engineer was down in the engine-room, beneath our feet. Sometimes he came up to the mouth of his hatch, right before us, and gazed out mysteriously, almost like an animal — like a woodchuck in its hole — at the waves astern of us. I suspect he wasn't enjoying it much. Perhaps none of them were enjoying it; they were doing what they had to do. But to us carefree passengers it was beautiful and thrilling. The waves dashed on the boat and raced back along our sides, all foam and water, white and blue (they were white and blue to my eyes, that is, but since then I have come to know a young Greek painter, Themos Maïpas, who conveys such wild waves uncannily, and he sees all kinds of colors in them — pink, ruby, violet, many greens and many browns — as well).

On reaching Amorgos we passengers went ashore, for a drink, and on the solid ground we staggered crazily. We lay in port there over night, and the ladies hoped for a longer respite, but the captain took off at dawn without consulting us, a deed for which he later apologized. He was anxious to get home. He had dragged his feet on the outward voyage, by and large, but now he was like a horse, with ears pricked forward, that is headed for its stable; and we made no really lingering calls thereafter.

On Saturday we had a fair amount of wind, but it was less than Friday's partly because we were in the Cyclades by then. That day at noon we stopped briefly at Naxos, a big and interesting island, with traces of strong Venetian-Catholic influence in its seaport town. Then at night we lay at Syra, which is the Cyclades's capital, their main port economically, and a famous source of *loukoumia*, the gelatinous candy that we call Turkish delight.

On Sunday we merely puttered along, stopping at a couple of beaches and staying in close range of the Piraeus, which the captain was bound to make that afternoon, and did. He had a tight schedule, and he had often been terrified, I imagine, of being late for the next charter.

After that cruise I went on living in Kifissia — its coolness being very welcome now — but I came to the city often. I would come down by a small electric train, and once in Athens I would head for Constitution Square — Plateia Syntagmatos — which is the center of Greek tourist life. "Tourism" was in full blast by then — in June — having built up through the spring. In winter the Greek weather can be stormy, and only stray tourists are about, random people en route to somewhere else — in my observation many more are seen in Egypt and India then. Easter is the real start of Greece's season — a number of people come then, and they keep coming, more and more, as the season wears on. By that June they had changed the city's aspect, or that of Constitution Square — it was adorned with tourists for the summer, one might say, as gardens are adorned with flowers. And I myself had become

a tourist-watcher, my focus shifting from the mountainsides to them.

At no time are the tourists in Greece as many as those in
France or Italy, say, but they have been increasing fast and
steadily. The Greek government pays much attention to
them, hoping that tourist income will fill ever more of the
deficit in their country's trade balance. Greece is not a rich
producer, and she must buy more goods, in value, than she
sells, a discrepancy covered in the past by things like shipping revenues, American aid, and family remittances from
the hordes of Greeks overseas. None of these incomes is
necessarily stable, and it is thought that a flourishing tourism will counteract any drops in them, as well as fattening
the budget generally. The government woos tourists, therefore, and it has a headlong program of building roads, hotels,
etc. to that end. Figures can be had on all aspects of the
phenomenon, but I shall quote only one here — I was told
that summer, by someone in our Athens consulate, that
10,500 Americans had entered Greece in July. This figure
had meaning statistically, of course, but it was hard for me
to visualize. I found it easier to sit in Constitution Square,
in June, and observe that the tourists were really swarming
there.

The square is a big one, oblong, and running down a slope
on its longer axis. The Greek Parliament is on its upper
end, but otherwise the place is given over to commerce.
Two of the city's five big cosmopolitan hotels are on the
square, and two more are within a block of it. The big travel
agencies are on it. So are several airline offices, the leading
international bookshop, and four or five cafés of which only
two are native enough to serve Turkish coffee, which the
Greeks themselves drink — they often call it "Greek" coffee, out of nationalism, but it is still the good old Middle

Eastern stuff, with grounds in the bottom. (The other cafés serve only traditional Western coffee — which they ominously, but not misleadingly, call "French" coffee — and the strange new drink of Nescafé, which is popular nowadays where tourists gather.)

In June the square was dead from two to five in the afternoons, for the Greeks took a siesta then, and all Athens was a glaring emptiness. But in the forenoons, and especially in the evenings, it was lively. In the forenoons tourists were out doing the errands that cannot be separated from their form of relaxation — they were checking on reservations, that is, buying souvenirs, mailing postcards, arranging for trips, and getting into cars or buses to take them. Most of these activities can be done on the square's north side, along a stretch of sidewalk on which front, in that order, the Hotel Grande Bretagne, the King George Hotel, a Greek café, a street intersection, a bookstore, a small curiosity shop, and the Athens branch of the American Express Company. From the door of the Grande Bretagne to that of the American Express is about a hundred yards, and at almost any midday in June this stretch held dozens of tourists, either in motion or sitting at sidewalk tables. Often they carried guide-books or cameras; they wore cool summer clothing with a foreign look; and they were altogether so different from Greeks that they could be spotted from afar by the guides, salesmen, and other sharpers who also held forth in that territory. Most of these latter wore business suits and looked like innocent bystanders, but a few bore the trappings of their trade. The one or two pistachio-nut vendors in the crowd, for instance, had big baskets on their arms, these containing many transparent packages of their wares. The one or two sponge salesmen, yet more spectacular, carried sponges strung together in two great lumps and hung from their shoulders, so that the entire mass, of man and merchandise, was wider than it was high. Most of the salesmen waited fairly motionless on the sidewalk, and the tourists hurried or sauntered past them, often greeting each other. The salesmen tried, meanwhile, to waylay them; and the sun played brilliantly on the busy scene.

In the June evenings the square would be calmer, but no less crowded. The tourists would be early at the cafés — say seven o'clock — then a good deal later the Greeks themselves would appear, in force. The Athenians live a double day, especially in summer. They rise early, work all morning, have a latish lunch — and perhaps a heavy one — subside for a few hours, work again in the early evening, then appear on the street at nine or so, to promenade or sit awhile till dinner time, which may not be till eleven. Thus they enjoy the cool of the night — they often dine out of doors — while immuring themselves through the day's worst heat. It is a pleasant system, the fruit of long experience, but it is a hard one for the tourists, most of whom are Northerners — there are few Italians among them, for instance — to adapt to. No matter how much they may delay in going to a *taverna* for dinner, and no matter how much they may linger there — no matter how wildly late, that is, they may think themselves in rising from the table — they usually meet a stream of Athenians entering as they pass out.

There are, as luck would have it, many good *tavernas* near Constitution Square, most of them in the Plaka, the oldest section of modern Athens, which lies in the half-mile between the square and the Acropolis. These *tavernas* have good Greek food and wine, some Greek popular music as a rule, and pleasant gardens that are cool in summer. They are only a fifteen-minute walk, say, from the hotels where tourists normally stay, and they always have people in them who speak English. Language is not a great factor with them anyway, for they follow the Greek *taverna* system of letting customers choose their food directly, from the stove or icebox.

The night-life in and around the square is special. There are several little night clubs in the area, most of them, however, being mere clip-joints where lone men are encouraged to buy drinks, real or fake, for the house girls — a truly clippable man may stay in a joint until it closes, on the expectation that the girl he is buying for will leave with him. Such places are inconspicuous holes in the wall, for the most part, and some of them keep runners out around the square to rustle up business. After midnight the square gets more and more deserted, and the crowd thins down to a few such runners plus a few girls themselves, perhaps, a policeman or two, and a few late-prowling customers.

As far as more formal, routine night-clubbing is concerned, there is a certain amount of it in Athens, but except for the so-called *bouzouki* establishments — and one *taverna* specializing in the music of Hadjidakis, the Greek hit king — it is much like night-clubbing anywhere.

One notable set of evening entertainments, though — the theater festival at Epidaurus — takes place near Athens in the early summer, after the start of the tourist season, for which it is especially designed. In 1959 I had taken in a couple of plays at Epidaurus, and late the next June I went to another. I had become still more of a tourist by that time, as I had been joined by my son Dick and his friend John Belmont, both of them twenty-one. I wanted to show Greece to them as well as to myself, and this gave a boost to my sightseeing. Epidaurus is forty-five miles from Athens as the crow flies. In classical times it was a sanctuary of

Asclepius, which included a theater that was thought out-standing then and has meanwhile suffered little damage. In June and July, when the days are long, the Greek National Theater Company puts on a few ancient plays there. I had seen the *Antigone* of Sophocles and the *Frogs* of Aristopha-nes the year before, and this year we saw the *Oedipus Rex* of Sophocles.

The three of us went to Epidaurus mainly by sea (another way to go is wholly by road, which takes a few hours each way and can be trying on the night return). Our boat, laid on especially and crammed with festival-goers, left the Piraeus at three o'clock and took two hours to reach the coast of the Peloponnesus, near Epidaurus, where we got off. The boat — perhaps it should be called a launch — was fast; it went like a torpedo; and it left a beautiful foamy, symmetrical, sculptured wake behind it. After landing we had time for refreshments at the seaport village, then we were all loaded onto buses — ten or twenty of them, very well organized — and carried through the landscape, for half an hour, to the Asclepius shrine. There we had a chance for further refreshments — I had wine and sandwiches — before going on to the theater, which was a few minutes' walk from the parking space.

We had reserved places rather high up, and we sat there on the old stone seats. The evening was soft, and the blue sky was darkening as we got there. The theater was half full by then — its capacity is fourteen thousand — and peo-ple were still drifting into it, quietly. The structure was a perfect bowl, or a perfect half-bowl, rather — its seats curved around to fill just over a hundred and eighty de-grees, and the remainder was left open. Through that space one saw the scenery of Greece. There was a grove of pines behind the stage, then some hills covered with a green

scrub, then a few tawny fields in the middle distance, and
finally an almost bare gray ridge — of limestone, apparently
— against the horizon; its silhouette was sharp in the evening sky. We were really out in nature. The air was still,
the countryside was still — I have heard that donkeys are
removed from the neighborhood while the festival is on —
and dusk was falling. The play began, and spotlights were
turned on here and there, but real dark was some distance
off. The round amphitheater converged on the "orchestra,"
a likewise round area, of earth, with the stage behind it,
on which the chorus soon began to move.

For those who don't know Greek the chorus is most
important in these Epidaurus productions. One can read
a play ahead of time — and Greek tragedies are short — so
that one can follow the action; but still the words, and
their delivery, can hardly fascinate if one doesn't understand them. The chorus, though, is mainly visual, and into
its motions have gone much contemporary Greek thought
— how the old Greek choruses moved (if they did move)
is unknown, and the Epidaurus choreography is modern.
The *Oedipus* chorus was made up of fifteen Theban men,
wearing gowns of a dull green. As the play unwound
they moved almost constantly down on the orchestra —
but moved slowly, sometimes almost imperceptibly. They
shifted, circled, passed through each other, paused, grouped,
and regrouped; and in their movements, and their voices
too, they reflected the play's moods, of excitement, sad-
ness, or expectancy. They kept changing delicately, like
water with a breeze on it. Sometimes they were in one
group, sometimes two, sometimes more, and they had a
leader who was often apart. They sighed, they stalked,
when the main actors were speaking, and when speaking
themselves they chanted, they almost sang. Meanwhile we

were out in nature still. A bat flew near me, and the mountain in the distance kept on changing. At half past eight it was purple, with the sky above it pink. The amphitheater itself (which had superb acoustics) fitted naturally into the bowl of a hill — the top row of stone seats, I noticed, led smoothly and perfectly to the bushy height above them. The play went on, with Oedipus and Jocasta unraveling their fates, on the stage, and defying oracles. Tiresias, the blind seer, was led in by a boy, and he too was defied, and he left. The chorus kept on moving, and it showed alarm and awe. It made the play dramatic, and for me it brought out the religious, ritualistic side as well. But as a ritual it was neither long nor tedious, and it ended in little over an hour. Oedipus blinded himself and was led off by his daughters. Later there was a curtain-call, and then we walked away through the night. We rolled off in our buses, we transferred to our boat with great dispatch, we had further wine and sandwiches in its saloon, and soon after midnight we were back in Athens.

Sophocles' *Antigone*, which I had seen the year before, was much the same in character, and I think this is true of all the tragedies put on at Epidaurus — with allowances for Aeschylus being more austere than Sophocles, and Euripides being less so. Some foreign purists in Greece say that the Epidaurus productions are sentimentalized — that having Oedipus led off by his little daughters, for instance, which has no textual authority behind it, is too tear-jerking. I can only say that it jerked no unwarranted tears from me, and that it seemed in keeping with the Oedipus legend and with the tragedy's own pitch — at its end, one must remember, Oedipus has just blinded himself, gorily and with thorough textual authority, after which the mere leading off by daughters seems, to me, a casual detail.

I have also heard the language of the plays criticized by these same purists. The texts are all translated into modern demotic Greek, and the purists say that this is done with a zeal that makes them commonplace at times. I can give no opinion on that point, but I can say that the plays are popular with many educated Greeks, and appear to be much respected by them.

Comedies are more chancy. With a few exceptions the old Greek comedies we have are by Aristophanes, and his works can't be given now in their original form. For one thing they are too obscene by modern standards — they are full of jokes about yellowing one's pants through fear, and things like that. They are also cluttered with obscure topical references. Even Plutarch, who lived only five centuries after Aristophanes, said that "if you recite him at a feast, each guest must have a grammarian beside him to explain the allusions." For these reasons old comedies have to be largely rewritten for Epidaurus, which may or may not turn out well.

I had good luck in that I saw the *Frogs*. It had enchanting fanciful choruses — that of the frogs themselves was superbly costumed and full of subtle antics. Then the play's climax, a contest between Aeschylus and Euripides, was delightfully handled — though not authentically so, except in spirit. In the play Sophocles has just died, and Dionysus, the God of the theater, goes to the underworld to bring back one of the two other great tragedians, both of whom are already there. He stages a contest, which Aeschylus finally wins (Aristophanes, a conservative, abhorred the likes of Euripides). At Epidaurus, Euripides was thin, pale, nervous, dirty, scratchy, and disreputable, while Aeschylus was more on the lines of General Eisenhower with a white beard. The two spent a long time lampooning each other's

works, and Aeschylus finally broke into a calypso tune, and
did a shimmy, in reciting what he felt was his rival's trashiest
line. It was just a fleeting touch, but it brought down the
house — or would have brought down a flimsier one — and
to me it seemed a perfect job of modernization. On the other
hand, the *Birds* of Aristophanes was put on that same year,
in Athens, and is said to have been a flop in many respects
— it was immediately closed by the government, among
other things, for being disrespectful to the Orthodox
Church.

There is another entertainment that we went to in June
that is worth noting here — some Greek folk-dances staged
in an old theater at the Piraeus. Most of them were expertly
done — costumes, music, and dancing seemingly perfect —
but I felt that this perfection was almost a flaw. The dancers
concerned were virtually a professional troupe, I gathered
— who had been doing the same thing, in the Piraeus, for
a long time — and I preferred a small section of the program that was put on by relative amateurs just in from one
of the islands.

Their performance had more roughness, but also more
vitality and *joie de vivre*. Later in the summer I saw folk-
dancing *in situ* in the islands, too, and I liked that still more,
even though there was no fancy dress then, and not much
polish in the steps. The Greek life and landscape have a
coarse and grainy texture much of the time, and if you
smooth it out you court disaster.

THE BIG LAND TOUR

In Dry Greece the most popular ruins, with tourists, are in Athens, Delphi, Olympia, and the region of Corinth and Mycenae. These places are so disposed that one can easily make a four-day circuit of them by car or bus, and each year many thousands do so. In June, I joined them, along with Dick and John Belmont — we went on rubberneck buses belonging to one of the main Greek tourist outfits.

I should say right now that I am partial to guided tours. Some friends of mine disdain them, and other people have done so at least since Cicero's time. But I have found them the best way to take in antiquities without devoting one's life to them and becoming a scholar. I don't like visiting ruins with a guidebook, as it keeps me from looking around — a classic joke about German tourists is that they never actually see the ruins they visit, because of guidebooks held pedantically before their eyes. The words and dates that go with ruins should come through the ears, and that is what live guides are for. It is true that one occasionally gets wrong information — old wives' tales — from some of them, and that nothing is more deadly than a guide who is stupid or cynical. But in Greece the stupidity, at least, is at a

minimum. In some countries the tourist guides are no better
than whining beggars, but in Greece, where nearly everyone is alert and intelligent, the guides are especially so.

Most of the good ones are women — guiding is one of
the few higher Greek callings really open to them. They
bring to it the lovely manners that all Greek women seem
to have, plus a great fluency in languages. Before they are
licensed they must have a schooling in archaeology. Then
as the years pass they learn more about it, and also perfect
their tact in handling the tourists themselves, a job demand-
ing the qualities of a teacher, nurse, mother, diplomat's wife,
and geisha girl. They make fine company, as well as being
instructive.

For conveyance around the big loop of ancient sites you
may use your own car, of course, if you have one. You may
hire a car in Athens, and I did this later in the year — it was
a Volkswagen, and with gas and everything it cost less than
a hundred dollars for the circuit. You may also hire a car
with a chauffeur — and even with a chauffeur who is a
guide of sorts himself. I know one guide-chauffeur in
Athens, named John Spyrakis, who has a Cadillac sedan and
a series of warm testimonials from Edith Hamilton, Vivien
Leigh, Sir Laurence Olivier, Graham Greene, Igor Stravin-
sky, and others. I have been out with him on an overnight
trip and have found him a charming man with a great feeling for the Greek past, but his foreign languages are so
limited that one cannot learn much from him. It is better to
have a really professional licensed-guide to tell you things.
You can hire such a guide all for yourself, and that is the
best way, but it is cheaper to take a rubberneck bus, which
costs only fifty-five dollars, everything included, for this
particular four-day trip.

Ideally one should stay with the same bus and the same

guide — getting to know him or her — throughout such a trip, and that is the way it used to be managed by the companies on the circuit. But in 1960 the particular company that I chose launched what I call an inferior system — a fact that I didn't realize till I had bought the tickets and we were on our way. The fault in the system came from applying mass-production, impersonal, "efficient" methods to the handling of tourists, a temptation that seems to arise when those in charge start thinking abstractly in terms of "tourism" rather than concretely in terms of satisfying people. As the tour business has evolved in Greece it has worked out that several lesser bus-trips, besides the big four-day one, are available on this main classical circuit. From Athens, the base for excursions in Greece, you can take a hasty one-day trip to Delphi or to Corinth and Mycenae, which are the circuit's two ends. Or you can take two-day trips to those places, staying overnight and seeing them at more leisure. In 1959, when visiting Greece with another son — Peter — I took two-day trips in both directions and got a great deal out of them. On the trip to Delphi, especially, we were guided by a delightful elderly Greek lady whom we came to know quite well. She took us around thoroughly in the cool times of day — late afternoon and early morning. She spent the evening with us. And then and in the bus itself she told us all manner of things. We felt our time had been excellently spent. But now it was hard to spend much of the time well, for this company's new system sought to combine their four-day tour with their one- and two-day tours at each end — the clients getting on and off like railway passengers — in such a way that "efficiency" was served, but few customers — few four-day customers at least — were really pleased. We kept being rushed to keep up with one-day people, or left to wait for someone else, and this took away from what was otherwise a pleasant experience.

We drove off from Constitution Square at eight on a Monday morning — at quarter past eight, more exactly, because of the difficulty in rounding all the passengers up and installing them. Our bus was a "pullman," with adjustable seats, a public-address system, and blue-tinted windows curving up over our heads. The dashboard looked, to me, like the instrument panel on a plane. The guide — it was a man on this first leg of the trip — sat up forward beside the driver. His microphone snaked in and out of a socket just in front of him, so that he could readily pick it up, say *f-f-f, f-f-f* into it (*φ-φ-φ, φ-φ-φ*, that is, in Greek), and begin his talks.

These turned out to be not especially good, as such things go, for though the guide was a capable man he seemed to be stale on tourists. Tourists *en masse* can be disillusioning. Often they tire easily. They have odd whims. Many care little for the sights they see, but just want to say they've seen them. And they ask extraordinary questions — "What are sponges used for?" I heard an old lady ask a guide last summer. Male guides especially, it seems, get impatient with this sort of thing and grow frivolous. As we spun along now, leaving Athens for the country, this guide pointed out the many olive trees around us, green in the light-brown grass. "The olive was Athena's divine gift to Athens," he said. "We use it for everything. We eat it, we cook with it, and its wood keeps us warm in winter. In Greece we eat ripe olives as a rule, but in dry martinis people use green ones. . . ." Then he did some dated joking about how little vermouth a dry martini should have.

Later we passed near a bauxite mine, and he began talking

about "aluminum" and "aluminium" and the differences between the English and American languages. "The word
'dame' means quite different things in English and American," he said. "I found that out in London a few years
ago. It was very embarrassing."

These quips, coming over the public-address system,
were interlarded with more serious comments.

A few miles out of Athens we stopped at the Byzantine
church of Daphni, which contains some famous mosaics.
The guide led us off the bus and brought us, like sheep, to
the church's courtyard. "This way, please," he said. "You
are better off in the shade." He got us to a cool spot and
gave a little speech on Daphni's history. In classical times
the place was a shrine of Apollo, he said, but the Huns
under Alaric destroyed it in the fourth century. Later on
— mainly in the eleventh century — the Byzantine Christians built their church there. "It was the golden age of the
Byzantines then," he said. "They were feeling so strong.
They were building for eternity."

He went on about the church's later adventures, which
included damage by the Crusaders; abandonment; part-
burial under silt; and eventual disinterment. While he was
talking a middle-aged lady slipped away from our group
and started for the church itself. "Excuse me, Madame,"
the guide called out. "Can we all wait here? Because others
are inside. We must all go in together." She came back
obediently.

The guide was right — there were a couple of groups
from other buses in the church, and the space there was
limited. But soon one group came out, and the guide cut
short his speech. "Well, ladies and gentlemen, here we go,"
he said. And he darted inside, with the rest of us following.

It was dark there, after the blazing sun, but still we could see the mosaics well. They were on the upper walls and the ceiling, in and under the dome. They had gleaming gold backgrounds, their colors were brilliant, and their execution polished; they are considered the finest Byzantine mosaics in Greece, indeed, on a par with those at Aghia Sophia in Istanbul. The guide began talking again, explaining the schism between the Orthodox and Catholic churches in the eleventh century. He did this lucidly, in both French and English — he had to say everything in both languages, because the passengers were mixed. I think his form was better in the French — I am not a good judge of that, but he seemed more at home in it.

After his general talk he began moving around and discussing the mosaics individually. One was of the Resurrection — a standard scene in Eastern iconography — and he gave a lively account of how it differed from Western versions of the same thing. In Western Resurrections, he explained, Christ is always ascending, but in the Greek ones he *de*scends to set free the old sinners — Adam and Eve and others — who are locked in the underworld. This was clearly shown in the mosaic, and the details of other scenes — the Baptism, Transfiguration, and so on — were clear too when he explained them.

He took us around for a while, then began shepherding us back to the bus. Several of us strayed off to buy postcards or soft drinks en route, and it was some time before he got us aboard and on our way.

We were heading for Delphi, which is seventy-five miles west of Athens as the crow flies, but which takes most of a morning to reach because of twisty mountain roads. We made only one more stop after Daphni, at a midpoint called Levadheia, where one can buy little *souvlakia* — spitted chunks of meat — flavored with oregano. We dawdled there awhile, but otherwise we spent the morning on our bus. The bus was cool, and coolly decorated, in blue and gray, a contrast to the glare outside. It had a radio, and up to Levadheia, when a tourist objected, this was playing soft, sweet music, which also made for a contrast — soft music within and hard landscape without — almost nothing there but rocky hills, with a sparse and sunburned vegetation. The tourist who objected was a Dutch professor, whom we came to know later on, and he complained bitterly, in French, that the music didn't harmonize with the *paysage*.

We pushed on silently into the burning country, dozing now and then because of its brightness. The guide didn't talk much. He identified some mountains that we passed — Cithaeron, where Oedipus was exposed as a baby, and Helicon, the home of the Muses — but otherwise he left us pretty much alone. I think the bilingual nature of the audience dampened him — at least it worked against spontaneity in him — for whatever he said in English he had to repeat in French, or vice versa, almost word for word, lest some of his passengers feel cheated. Later on, at Delphi, a French-speaking woman attacked him heatedly for saying more in English than in her language. The charge was groundless, but that did not abate her fury; and since then other guides, of more established position, have told me that they will not go on these bus-trips because the bilingual work is so trying.

The mountains were rocky, and they grew wilder, grander, and more rugged as we went along. Toward noon we came in sight of Parnassus, under which Delphi lies. It was massive and laced with gorges, some of which, high up, had snow on them. We reached the mountain's foot, then ran along its south side for a long time — slowly, over curving roads and switchbacks — till at length we came to Delphi itself, which hangs above a lovely chasm. The bus dropped us at the Hotel Delphi for lunch, immediately after which we were scooped up again and taken to see the ruins — hastily, so that the one-day tourists among us could get back to Athens. We four-day customers were due to spend the night in that hotel, but the check-out time was three p.m., and we couldn't get into our rooms yet.

Our guided tour of Delphi left much to be desired because it was so rushed. The guide did a brave job — talking rapidly in both languages, and even answering questions if driven to — but he had to leave at half past three, with the one-day people, and he could only hit the high spots. It was a poor hour to be seeing things too — hot and glary, with everything looking at its deadest. (It was also an hour, of course, when most of the Greeks themselves were secluded indoors.) I did little more than tag along on the tour — not absorbing much — and I got the guide to arrange for another man, a local guide in Delphi, to take the boys and myself around after five o'clock.

Of all the classical sites in mainland Greece I think Delphi is the most interesting and beautiful, and when living in Athens I have urged visiting friends to see it if they could see nothing else (Athens itself being excepted from this rule, as visitors go there automatically). Delphi's relation to old Greek life is easier to grasp than that of other shrines. Many Greek shrines were places where pilgrims went for formal worship, apparently, and not much else; and it is hard now to tell just what this meant to them. But Delphi, besides having the formal worship, also had the Oracle, to which questions came from far and wide and were answered; and in the best period of Greece, at least, the answers were generally heeded. The Oracle started wars, composed disputes, and told where colonies should be founded; and it governed many smaller things as well. Its statements — made by a medium, in a trance, and then interpreted by priests — were often ambiguous and sometimes crookedly reported, because of bribery, but they closely influenced their world, almost as much as the pronouncements of Marxism and Catholicism influence their respective worlds today — though with the difference that they were not codified. They were the unpredictable voice of the God, Apollo — of the wind blowing where it listeth — but they had great practical effects. These can be studied and learned about — there is a lot on them in Herodotus, for instance — and the knowledge helps make Delphi seem alive.

As for the place's beauty, this lies mainly in its site, with Parnassus towering above it and the deep gorge lying down below, carpeted with an absolute sea of olive trees — over a million of them, according to the guides. The shrine is just north of the Corinthian Gulf. Most of its view in that direction is blocked by a rugged height to its south, but around one end of this, and far below, an arm of the Gulf is visible — the so-called bay of Itea — and it gives the scene a dash of water to set it off.

Everywhere there is a sense of space. From Delphi itself one looks across the gorge and sees a footpath zigging and zagging — at a constant pitch, and with sharp and equal angles in its switchbacks — up the facing heights. It looks almost like a work of mechanical drawing, and one sees it ever so clearly; but in between are volumes of crystal air. The crags to Delphi's rear are wild and lovely, too, and the remains of the shrine itself — which include a stadium, a theater, parts of two temples, and some other buildings — are as enjoyable as any in Greece. They were excavated

early in this century by French archaeologists, after the
modern village of Delphi, which stood on them, had been
removed — it is now five or ten minutes' walk away, along
the hillside. There is a good museum at Delphi, too — still
being improved as this is written — and on every count it
is an excellent place to visit.

We met our guide in front of the museum, and for five
dollars he agreed to take us in hand for a couple of hours.
His card bore the legend "PANAGHIOS GERCUSIS,
Speaker on Delphi," and the phrase was apt. He was a
portly man, of middle height. He wore dark glasses and a
straw hat. He was a compulsive talker, and when he had
seated us on some old chunks of marble he began narrating
at once with wild surmise.

"The primitive people who lived here in the beginning,"
he said, with a rolling brogue, "started to worship the infer-
r-r-rnal beings. They worshipped the earth Goddess. They
worshipped Gaea, who was the same as Isis. They worshipped Rhea, who was also Goddess of the earth. And
Poseidon, the God of springs. He represented humidity!
They worshipped the dark, and moisture, and the full-of-
sickness powers of the earth. The microbes!"

He went on, retelling ancient myths and talking of a
python that supposedly had been at Delphi in those early
days. Then he pointed to the sky. "But in time Apollo, the
God of light, came and killed the python," he said. "That
was the triumph of light over darkness — Apollo with his
bright rays destroyed the dark!! The victory symbolized
the downfall, too, of the matriarchal system, which had
prevailed in Greece up to then."

He moved on to the Oracle. "In the historical period the
Oracle lasted exactly one thousand year-r-r-rs," he said.
His brogue was pronounced, and I found out later that he

had got a type of British accent from studying at an Anglican school in Jerusalem. He had been brought up there, the ward of a relative in the Greek Patriarchate, though his family home was Crete. He had traveled a good deal, too, before coming to rest in Delphi. Now he owned some olive trees in the gorge, which he cared for in the off season; but speaking on Delphi was his real job. He spoke in splendid periods, and he waved his arms.

He told how the medium of the Oracle, a woman, used to sit on a tripod over a cleft in the earth and make cryptic utterances. At first she was always a young virgin, he said, but then "something happened with a priest," and thereafter she was a woman over fifty. Her utterances were interpreted by a priestly corps — "twenty-four of them, all philosophers" — who came to have great influence.

"They had a peace policy," he said, "and they favored the unity of Greece. They developed the Amphictyonic League in Delphi, which was the forerunner of the UN." He quoted some of the famous oracles, like the one referring to Athens's wooden wall, which led her to rely on the fleet that beat the Persians. He recited these oracles, ringingly, in the ancient words. He furrowed his brow, he peered at us, he waved a finger, he leaned forward. He was a natural raconteur. He told us how Apollo had reigned at Delphi only half the year, yielding it to Dionysus in the winter. "Dionysus is the God of wine," he said, "and we drink in the winter. We do it now. It is cold in Delphi then, and we cannot work. So we stay home with our wine and worship Dionysus." And he laughed.

During this discourse we had been sitting on old blocks of marble — Dicky on a drum from an Ionic column — by the entrance to the sanctuary, which is at its lower end and near the modern road and museum. Now we rose and proceeded up the slope, up steps. Delphi was long ago stripped, by the Byzantines and others, but in its heyday it was full of statues and other votive offerings, given by people who wished to thank or please Apollo. "From the sixth century B.C.," the guide said, "when this place started to flourish, it *gleamed* with votive offerings. With gold, brass, bronze, and shining marble!"

All that was left of these objects now was their background of weathered stone, but he did a good job of conjuring up the ancient splendor. It was not just showmanship and talk, either, so far as I could tell, but an outpouring of pretty solid knowledge. The guide was well versed in Pausanias and he also went into such matters as the etymology of Delphi's name — into whether or not it came from a word meaning dolphin, as many people say (with the explanation that Apollo was brought to the site by a dolphin, or came in the guise of one himself). The guide was not dogmatic on such points. "We do not know anything," he said once. "What do we know? We know nothing." And in this mood he showed us over the sanctuary, including the cleft from which the Oracle had spoken, while the heights across the gorge turned red in the sunset.

We spent that night in the Hotel Delphi, which was a pleasure. Many new tourist hotels are being built in Greece now. Some are trite in design and some are good, and of the good ones the Hotel Delphi is outstanding. The architect seems to have been under Japanese influence. The balconies are reminiscent of Japan, and so is the layout of the rooms and corridors. Above all, the close connection between indoors and out seems Japanese. Thanks to the artful placing of terraces, balconies, and windows an inmate of the hotel is not debarred, as in so much Western building,

from communion with the landscape; and this is a boon because that landscape is so magnificent. You can eat, sleep,
and wake in the hotel, and stay in touch the while with the
rocky heights, the deep gorge, and the gorge's nap of olive
trees.

One would like to say that the food was equally good,
but this is impossible — one cannot praise the food in any
first-class hotel I know of on these tourist routes. If one is
on a package tour, as we were now, one gets table d'hôte
fare in the hotels, as part of the over-all deal, and this nearly
always consists of bland and listless imitations of the Western
cuisine. One could do that whole big loop of sightseeing
and come away quite knowledgeable on ruins, perhaps, but
unaware that Greeks eat palatable food. One is fed a round
of beef stews, dull beige soups, overdone roasts, and anemic
fish fillets on the theory, no doubt, that such things are the
least common denominator of food — that no guest will
object to them very much. To me that diet is associated with
the bureaucratic approach typified by the word "tourism"
— the approach that treats wayfarers like statistical units
rather than humans.

A more amusing sign of that approach, too, can be seen
in the same hotel. When we took possession of our rooms
we found big paper seals, saying "STERILIZED" in English, fixed to the covers of the toilet seats. They were im-
pressive, but I happened to know they were meaningless,
because the year before, when staying at that hotel, I had
left my room at the last moment — check-out time — had
gone out to my bus, then had remembered a book I had
forgotten, and had returned to get it; I had found the maid
and a manservant making the room up hastily, and they had
already put a crisp new "STERILIZED" sign on the toilet.
The more "tourism" gets organized, one imagines, the more
can tourists look forward to such minor insults.

But at that hotel the pleasantness of the surroundings
more than balanced off the nonsense, and besides we could
get good potable wine — as one can anywhere in Greece
— to liven up the food. Being with the tourists now — not
with the shepherds and the fishermen — I was often to be
cut off from the free-flowing *retsina* of my springtime, yet
at several hotels, I found, I could still get house wine in
carafes, and at all I could get labeled wine for prices starting around fifty cents a bottle. Greek wines don't make
connoisseurs rave, but they are recognized as good stuff in
an unpretentious way. They are in the shadow of French
and other European wines, and they concede this by the
shape of their bottles, among other things. Bordeaux-type
wines, both red and white, come in light, relatively square-
shouldered bottles; Burgundy types come in heavier, more
sloping ones; and Rhine wines in slopinger ones still. There
is much variety in all these categories, and no visitor, whatever his tastes, need go thirsty. Greece has some good
dessert wines, too, including a delicate muscatel made on
Samos.

The country offers a wide gamut for the serious drinker.
Besides all the wines (and imported liquors, of course, which
are expensive) there is a tasty local beer, a number of local
brandies, and infinite kinds of *ouzo*, the liquor that is the
common man's café drink. The beer, a monopoly, is called
ΦΙΞ or "FIX," after a brewmaster named Fuchs who was
imported to Greece in the nineteenth century, following
her liberation from Turkey, by the Bavarian royal house
that was chosen to rule her then. It is one of the best lagers
made in the Mediterranean region (another being the Dutch
Amstel beer now brewed in Jordan). The brandies, called
koniak in Greek, are rather special; they taste good to those
who like them, but simultaneously sweet and harsh to those
who don't. The *ouzo* is a member of the family that includes

anisette, absinthe, pernod, raki, and *arak*. It is distilled, theoretically at least, from the leavings in the wine-presses; it
turns white in water; and it has an anise taste. A drink of it
costs five or ten cents in ordinary Greek cafés, but closer to
twenty-five in high-class hotels, where it is not allowed to
undersell gin and whiskey too drastically. Rivers of *ouzo*
are drunk in Greece, but one also hears some calumny
about it there, perhaps derived from snobbishness.

"I disapprove of *ouzo*," a Greek friend said to me one
evening last year.

"Why?" I asked.

"It goes to the head," he answered sternly. Whereupon
he poured himself a huge, mahogany-colored scotch and
soda, though where that was going I did not ask.

Another time a Greek barfly saw me drinking *ouzo* in a
hotel and lectured me about it with the strange emphasis
that people sometimes display in bars. He too was drinking
scotch, and he had an intent look. He said *ouzo* was dangerous in quantity, though safe if taken only now and then.

"You mean it's all right if one doesn't live on the stuff?"
I asked.

"It's not a question of living on the stuff!" he said furi-
ously. "But simply of not drinking too much of it!!!"

He added that a surfeit of *ouzo* had given *him* internal
spasms. I have downed a fair amount of it, though, and have
found it no more sinister than other hard liquors — perhaps less so, as it is apt to be weaker.

We rose early after our night at Delphi, to catch a ferry
across the Gulf of Corinth. Our numbers were reduced
now, by the defection of the one- and two-day people, and
we were loaded into a half-sized bus — a Volkswagen or
something similar. We tourists were fourteen in number.

Besides the boys and myself we had the Dutch professor
and his wife, a French businessman and his wife, two French-
speaking single women (of whom at least one was Swiss),
an elderly Greek-American from Maryland, and a family
group from Chicago consisting of a grandfather, his
daughter, and her two teen-age sons. These last were too
young to enjoy the trip much — they seemed to have been
dragged along, and they would sigh, and speak of baseball,
and wish it was all over. The two French-speaking ladies
seemed unhappy, too — one was old and not quite up to
the ardors of the trip, and the other it was who had so
angrily accused the guide, the day before, of favoritism to
English. All the rest of us, I should say, were keenly curious.
Except for the Greek-American we had the attitude of
ordinary well-educated Westerners now finally seeing the
things we had heard praised in school. The Greek-American
was different. He had gone to the States early in this century, as a poor boy, and had lived a hard life there, like
most Greek-Americans of his vintage. He had worked his
way up in the restaurant business and had finally come to
own a place of his own; but not till this year — he was now
well on in his sixties — had he had the time or money to
come back to his old country. Like many first-generation
Greek-Americans that one meets back in Greece, he was
both proud of the old country and appreciative of the
United States. He was soft-spoken and patient, and he kept
mainly to himself. The Greece of us others, around which
the tour had been built — the Greece of Homer and the
schoolroom busts — can have meant but little to him, yet
he seemed always interested and happy to be along. I know
that he was proud, too, of our respect for the Greek culture,
so different from what he must have found as an immigrant.

We had no guide on this leg — as part of the general

efficiency we were to have a stationary guide at Olympia
and not pick up another traveling one till the last day, in
the region of Corinth and Mycenae. We did have a "hostess,"
a young girl who was pleasant, but who lacked the com-
posure, knowledge, and linguistic ability that real guiding
needs, and of course we had a chauffeur — a good, tough
professional well able to cope with the mountain roads and
with the spirit of Greek traffic, which is still untamed and
scofflaw. We left the hotel, drove down the steeps through
olive groves to the bay of Itea, and boarded a ferry that
was, I think, an old American landing-craft from the
Second World War. We crossed the Gulf slantwise, going
many miles west as well as south, and the trip took us two
or three hours. In the course of it we met a school of
dolphins, and they played entrancingly around our bow —
leaping rhythmically from the water, going in pairs, crossing each other's track, and curvetting everywhere.

The ferry put us down on the Peloponnesus, the lower,
severed part of the Greek peninsula. We still had some distance to go before Olympia — west along the Gulf's south
coast, then south on the Adriatic shore, then inland for a
spurt. It is one of the duller routes in Greece, by and large,
and our hostess did not enliven it. We crossed about five
streams on the journey, and at each one she inquired its
name from the driver and then relayed it to us. She also
told us what the towns we passed exported, and this in-
variably was wine and olives. Otherwise she let us doze,
which was easy in the heat and brightness, and under the
fatigue of traveling. We dozed and waked. We saw blue
sea with the brown-green land beside it. We saw magpies
flying, black and white. We saw donkeys. We saw olive
trees floating in the tawny glare outside. We saw flashes of
bougainvillea in the towns. Then as the noon-hour passed

we saw shuttered houses locked in the siesta — saw people
sleeping on verandahs, too, in the hope of a breeze. Then
about one we made Olympia, where we were fed, allowed
to rest, and told that our guide would come at half past
three.

The guide was a woman this time; she had brown hair
and bright blue eyes, these made brighter still by a figured
blue dress she wore. She was brisk and full of vitality (a
thing that guides need badly, for if a guide wilts, the tourists
do the same). She was also on her mettle — almost hostile
at first — in anticipating complaints from us. She seemed
to be the anchorman, so to speak, of this tour system — the
one who took the heavy load of it half way through — and
I gathered she was used to customers who felt they had
been slighted earlier. "I tell you that you'll have a visit here
that you can't say was done in a hurry," she said with chal-
lenge in her eye, and she gathered us up and swept us off.

She took us first to the museum, which is near the hotel
at Olympia (the latter being a nice old-fashioned one, amid
quiet pines and gardens). The museum contains some outstanding pieces, including the Hermes of Praxiteles and the
pediment groups from both ends of the Olympian temple
of Zeus. It is hard to get excited over the Hermes, after all
the photographs one has seen of it, but still the quality of
the stone — a translucent, almost glowing white marble —
is a pleasant surprise, and so is the three-dimensional view
of the statue as one walks around it (it is mounted over
a bed of sand, in case it should topple in an earthquake, but
a wooden gangway is laid on this so one can circulate).

The pediment sculptures, rather archaic, are among the
least publicized of good Greek statues, and they are all the
more striking for that. One group shows the legend of
Pelops, for whom the Peloponnesus is named, and the other

the attempted abduction of Lapith women by Centaurs at
a wedding feast (the same story as is shown in the Parthenon
metopes at the British Museum). The Centaurs are full of
life, ruggedness, and primitive purpose, and they are at-
tacking the Lapith women and their protectors with direct
and practical holds and blows. In the center of the pediment — its tallest part — stands Apollo, the god of light,
with an arm outstretched, and in the triangle on either side
of him the struggle goes on, gradually working upward as
it comes toward him from the low corners. The guide
pointed out that the higher the contestants' figures rose,
and the nearer they got to Apollo, the more the virtuous
Lapith women seemed to be winning, and she drew a sym-
bolic meaning from the struggle — that the Lapiths stood
for the good forces in humanity and the Centaurs the bad;
and that people should, according to the pediment, always
strive to control the Centaur within them. (I have heard
this interpretation from others, too, and it strikingly recalls
the Hindu symbolism of that same inner struggle — the
metaphor of the charioteer in the Bhagavad Gita controlling
the wild horses of the senses.)

The guide also ascribed various thoughts to the figures in
the Pelops pediment. These stand in a row, and supposedly
they are waiting to begin a chariot race in which Pelops, according to the legend, won his bride by besting her father
through foul play. It was understood that Pelops would be
killed if he lost the race to the girl's father — who was king
of the region around Olympia — but he secretly bribed
the old man's groom to take the linch-pin out of his chariot
axle, thereby causing it to wreck. Pelops is made to seem
confident in the pediment, according to the guide, and so is
the girl, who knew about the trick. "Look at her," said

the guide. "See how calm she is. She can afford to be, be-cause she knows that Pelops is coming back." She told us what words the girl might be saying as they waited there, and what Pelops might be saying, too. It was rather like putting balloons in the mouths of figures in a painting, yet it was stimulating, and I think it made most of the tourists take more interest — even if this was the negative interest of objection.

The guide rather lent herself to controversy. One room in the museum held many statues from the Roman period, and she ran these down unmercifully. "The Romans were excellent at draperies, copies, and portraits," she said. "They were great at mass production. They mass produced the bodies of their statues and then put portrait heads on them. Sometimes the heads were out of proportion with the rest, but they didn't seem to mind that."

One tourist in our party took issue with the guide, but she was able to find examples to prove her point. She was quick at repartee, and not averse to it. "How often have I been called a nationalist in this same room," she said with spirit, as she led us from the Roman things.

By the time we left the museum it was reasonably cool outside, and she took us to the ruins of the sanctuary it-self, which — unlike Delphi's — are on a level space, amid pine trees. They include the remains of a temple to Zeus, of one to Hera, and of many other buildings, among them the old Olympic stadium. The guide got us around these well, giving full explanations and answering all our ques-tions, whether in French or English. She was a heroine of sorts. She drew us along from point to point, always getting to the next one before we did — sometimes she even ran, and she kept us on our toes. She said she had guided eleven

hundred tourists around Delphi since March fifteenth — it
was then the end of June. She was under contract to stay
there, working for our tour company, till mid-October, and
it seemed that they had made an excellent choice — no
matter what went wrong for a tourist on the rest of his trip,
it would always be plain that she, at least, meant business.

That evening the boys and I took a dip in the River Al-
pheus — cool, swift, and muddy — which runs past Olympia, then we had drinks and dinner and went to bed in the
quiet hotel. The next day we were not scheduled to leave
till afternoon, and I spent most of the morning in the sanctuary. As I have indicated, the function of this sanctuary
does not come over so clearly as that of Delphi's, at least to
me. Olympia was sacred pre-eminently to Zeus, he being
the great father-god of the Greeks — their Jehovah, perhaps — associated somehow with power as Apollo was with
light (it has been argued that the two later continued in
Christianity as God the Father and God the Son). Zeus's
shrine at Olympia seems to have been fully as international
— as common to all the Greek states — as was Apollo's at
Delphi, and the various Greeks would put aside their quar-
rels when they gathered for its festivals, among which the
Olympic games were a feature. Olympia had great prestige,
apparently, and majesty and formality. The sanctuary was
as big as a few city blocks. It was laid out on orderly rectangular lines, and these are still perceptible, though blurred
by the confusion in which the masonry has fallen — thanks
to earthquakes and other causes — through the years. The
place was silted over, additionally, by changes in the Al-
pheus and another river, and around its edges one can now
see earthen banks, ten or twenty feet high, marking the

depth through which German archaeologists dug down to
the ruins in the nineteenth century. Pine trees were later
planted, and these are tall now, so that the whole site lies
in a grove of them.

That morning, when I visited, the pines were roaring in
a wind, and they gave a welcome shade — a broken one, too,
with the sun's brilliance dappled by patches of shadow, all
superimposed on the ruins' pattern. There were wild pink
hollyhocks in the sanctuary, amid the brown grass, and they
nodded in the wind. There was Queen Anne's lace, too,
and other weeds. It was a scene of quiet, underlined by the
sighing of the trees.

Outstanding among the ruins was the temple of Zeus —
what was left of it — a big raised platform in the precinct's
center. It had been brought down largely by a single earthquake, and along one side a row of columns lay like tipped-
over stacks of checkers — drum after drum leaning on each
other. The drums were big, the base ones being a foot wider
than I am tall. They were of gray porous stone, with sea-
shells visible in it, and they had a rough texture brought out
by the slanting sun. They lay there in their grayness, amid
the pinkness of the hollyhocks and the toast-color of the
grass.

I wandered among them and then went to the other buildings — a Hera temple, which was a good deal smaller; the
remains of a workshop once used by Phidias; and so on.
Even toward noon it was cool and pleasant there. The pines
towered above, and once I saw a little owl flying among
them. It must have been young and inexperienced to be out
at all then. It stayed around for several minutes — flying
from tree to tree, and resting, then flying on again, softly in
the shadows, until it disappeared.

That afternoon we drove eastward across the Peloponnesus — "Pelops's Island" — mainly through the region
called Arcadia, which takes up most of its center. Arcadia
is wild and mountainous — good guerrilla country — and
in history its people have been self-reliant and hard to sub-
due. In ancient times they held out uncommonly well against
the neighboring Spartans, and in the nineteenth century
they were leaders in the anti-Turkish struggle. The road
across Arcadia crawls steeply up and down the mountains,
yet one does not feel shut in, for the views are generally
spacious — wide plains or valleys stretching from one's
own to other mountains, these being brown and green in
the distance. The trip took several hours, and we dozed and
chatted in the little bus, the same as had taken us from
Delphi — we had come to know each other pretty well by
now.

Toward dusk we reached Nauplion, a port on the east
Peloponnesian coast, where we were to spend the night.
It is an attractive town, with good swimming, interesting
medieval fortifications, and many handsome neo-classical
houses that were built in the first half of the nineteenth
century, when Nauplion was the capital, for a while, of
liberated Greece — Athens still being insecure then.

It is not for Nauplion itself that the tour buses stop there,
however, but for several ancient sites in its vicinity. The
next day we set forth to view them, though a bit confusedly
from having to mesh in with one- and two-day tourists
coming out from Athens. To one of the sites, called Tiryns,
we were not actually taken by the organized tour; but the
place is near Nauplion, and the boys and I went there in a
taxi, with the French couple, after breakfast. Then we came
back and joined the others, to be taken up to Mycenae in
a bus. The one-day pullman bus from Athens, with a guide,

was due to meet us there, but it was an hour late because it had to stop at Corinth on the way. Besides its one- and two-day tourists, apparently, it had some four-day ones who were going around the big circuit in a direction opposite to ours, and these had to see Corinth then or never, as it is midway on the Athens-Nauplion trip.

The people controlling our own movements did not know of this circumstance, so they sent us up an hour early. It was getting toward noon then, and very hot. Our bus stopped by some pine trees a good distance from the actual Mycenae ruins, and we were asked to wait there. We did wait for a while, sitting under the pines, but then grew restive. Some of us began wandering around to have a look. This alarmed the Greek driver of our bus, who had sole charge and who dreaded losing us — as those in charge of tourists always do. He enlisted the support of our Greek-American fellow-traveler, who tried to keep us still. But we were in no mood for this, and some of us answered to the general effect that we were not cattle and would do as we pleased. The Greek-American, caught in the middle of this argument, seemed unhappy. I felt he thought that we were being rude to his mother-country, or unappreciative of it — or perhaps that his countrymen themselves weren't cutting a good figure.

Any of these feelings would have been natural, but also unfounded as I saw it. I think one *can* say that the Greeks — to their vast credit, on the whole — are not yet organization men, and this works against them in big-scale tourist-shuffling enterprises. Otherwise I would put the blame for the mess that morning on a single wrong idea, which anyone might have had — the idea that a hitherto pleasant mode of touring should be streamlined and made efficient without heed to human values. (I suppose the com-

pany saved money by it, and this might be counted a gain
of sorts, yet real economic necessity cannot be argued, for
at least one other outfit was running four-day tours that
summer, at the same price, in the old well-timed, well-
guided way.)

The bus finally arrived, with a big complement of tourists
and a spunky little female guide. She took us first to a celebrated Mycenaean "bee-hive" tomb nearby and then to the
acropolis of Mycenae itself, briefing us at each in the usual
two languages. She didn't have time to say much, though,
or to take us thoroughly over the site; and anyway noon in
summer is a deadly moment to see that place. I prefer to
remember it from a visit I made later, in September. I went
there toward dusk that time, then returned in the evening
and saw it again by moonlight (I stayed overnight in the
neighborhood, at an inn that had once been the home of
Heinrich Schliemann, the archaeologist).

I had a better understanding of Mycenae by then, too,
having just visited Crete and having also looked over the
Mycenaean treasures in Athens, at the National Museum.
Thanks to Schliemann, and to archaeologists after him, we
know now that an advanced civilization existed in Greece
from about 1400 to 1150 B.C., long before the so-called
classical period. This older civilization is probably the one
that Homer wrote of — before Schliemann, Homer was not
much believed by modern scholars. It is at Mycenae itself
that the greatest finds from the civilization have been made;
and Mycenae also appears to have been its main center (as
witness the fact that Agamemnon, the Mycenaean king,
was leader of the Greeks at Troy). So the name "Mycenaean" has been given to the period, though many other
Greek towns flourished then as well — especially near the

coasts, for the civilization was maritime. It was derived in part from the Minoan civilization of Crete, also maritime, which had blossomed in the centuries just previous; and many similarities are found between Mycenaean objects and those unearthed at Cnossos — which include rich jewelry, for instance, seals, and mural paintings of thin-waisted youths and women. Archaeologists have been able, in fact, to date Mycenaean objects by their correspondences with Minoan ones, much as they earlier dated Minoan ones by their correspondences with Egyptian. It seems that civilizing tendencies were spreading northwestward in that second millennium B.C. — from the Nile to Crete and then to Greece itself.

The Minoan and Mycenaean styles co-existed for some time in the Aegean, with the former slowly waning and perhaps being overrun, in the end, by the latter. Two written languages of the second millennium have been found on Crete, the older called Linear A and the younger Linear B. The latter has also been found, in quantity, in Mycenaean sites on the mainland, and its recent decipherment has shown it to be Greek. This suggests that Greeks were dominant at Cnossos early in Linear B's heyday, which began in the fifteenth century.

Linear A, incidentally, has not yet been deciphered. Linear B was largely solved in the 1950's by a young British architect, Michael Ventris, who has since died. Though he found that the words in it were structurally Greek, the characters may have been borrowed from Linear A, which may or may not have been a local Cretan invention. The whole subject is still vague, and scholars are working hard on it. One main scene of their effort is at Pylos in the western Peloponnesus — at the palace of King Nestor, the Homeric

peacemaker — where an American archaeologist, Carl Ble-
gen, has made valuable finds including many of the tablets
from which Linear B was deciphered.

After the Mycenaean flowering, Linear B seems to have
dropped from use. Linguistically, at least, there may have
been a Greek dark age from then until the eighth century,
when writing started up again with an alphabet adapted
from the Phoenicians — this being the alphabet of classical
literature. The Mycenaean civilization is like a hidden room,
so to speak, lying behind the classical one and now being
slowly opened.

If you have all this in mind you can get more pleasure
from Mycenae. What you see there, aside from the tombs
— a remarkable engineering feat, done with huge, precisely
fitted blocks of stone — is the acropolis or citadel of the
old — presumably Homeric — city. This is a strong, brood-
ing place with a massive wall around it, and it sits on a height
near the pass that leads northward, toward Corinth, from
the so-called Plain of Argolis. It overlooks the whole plain,
too, which is not large — only about seven miles by nine —
but which in the Mycenaean age held two other citadels as
well, those of Tiryns and Argos. The former, which we
had visited earlier on that morning of the tour, is like Mycenae in character — strong, forbidding, and made of huge
stone blocks (the masonry is known technically as Cy-
clopean, from an old belief that only Cyclopes could have
put it together). The three citadels are but one or two
hours' walk from each other, yet in the Mycenaean age they
often warred. From Mycenae — looking down across the
plain to Nauplion, by a blue bay — one gets a sweeping
view of these international relations, and their small compass.
Then the bay itself, of course, leads off to the Aegean, over
which came and went the civilizing influences.

Mycenae has another set of associations — those involving the cursed family of Agamemnon — that affect some tourists deeply. According to legend Agamemnon returned from Troy only to be murdered by his wife Clytemnestra and her lover Aegisthus, his own first cousin. Then the guilty pair themselves were killed, in revenge, by Clytemnestra's son Orestes, at the urging of her daughter Electra. These deeds, so movingly dramatized by playwrights through the ages, were presumably done in Mycenae's citadel — some guides will even show you the bathroom floor where Agamemnon may have expired — and many visitors get an eerie feeling about the place because of this. Yet the deeds, assuming that they happened, took just a moment in the whole great history of the place, and I have always been more impressed with its calmness and impregnability. The last time I saw it, on that moonlit September night, it was quietness itself, sitting so pale and solid on its hilltop.

When the guide had shown us Mycenae, we boarded the bus, to return for lunch at Nauplion. We all held reserved seats, recorded on our tickets, and now we found that the same ones had been assigned, in many cases, to both one- and four-day tourists. We got over this mix-up amicably, however, and in the end I found myself sitting next to a red-haired Canadian girl, a secretary, who was in Greece for only a few days, as part of a European tour. She was confused as to her whereabouts, and as to the route the bus was following — someone had just told her, evidently, that the trip was a good way to spend a day — yet she was also friendly and intelligent, and I think she was having a good time. We chatted on till Nauplion. There the boys and I, old hands by now, managed to sneak in a swim before lunch.

Then we ate, afterwards getting into the bus again and heading for the sanctuary of Epidaurus, perhaps an hour to the east.

We three had already been there, a few days earlier, to the performance in the theater; but that had been in the evening, and we had seen little else. Epidaurus was actually the most important shrine, in ancient Greece, of Asclepius, the God of healing. From all directions Greeks went there for cures, much as people go to Lourdes today, and the sanctuary was a big place, with temples, related structures, and many votive offerings. The theater was an outstanding feature of the complex, and now the guide took us there to demonstrate its acoustics. She got us to go part way up in the tiers of semicircular seats, while she herself stood in the exact center of the chorus — the round space down below us — and dropped a coin, whose jingle we heard clearly. Then she spoke in a low voice, and we heard that. Then she began walking toward us, while speaking, and her voice faded out, as if she were going away. Acoustically the whole theater seemed to concentrate, perfectly, on that center point.

Later she took us to the museum, which contains inscriptions about cures as well as votive offerings — stone replicas of diseased or injured members of the body — left in the shrine by thankful patients. (The same thing is done in Greece today, though with silver replicas more often than stone, and I was to see much of it in August at a shrine on the isle of Tinos — to see silver plaques with reliefs of arms, legs, chests, or other members stamped in them, which had been left as thanks in the church there. And many other Greek churches contain such offerings.)

The methods of therapy used at Epidaurus are not well understood now, but they seem to have gone beyond pure faith healing. There was a large building in the sanctuary, near the Asclepius temple itself, and it is believed that visiting patients were told to sleep there on their first night and then report their dreams, which were used in diagnosis. It is also thought that the temple priests developed into rudimentary doctors as time passed — working up herbalism, and such material cures, in step with the priests at other Asclepius shrines — notably that on Kos, the home of Hippocrates.

There are many mysteries about it all. At Epidaurus there was an elegant *tholos*, or round building, of polished marble, designed in the Corinthian order by the architect who did the theater. Remains of this building can be seen in the museum now, and its foundation is intact outside, in the sanctuary. This foundation has concentric circular walls in it — about man high, as I remember them — with narrow doorways placed in each wall, these out of line in such a way that the whole cellar is a maze. Another guide once told me — on another occasion — that the cellar may have been used to house the sacred serpents of Asclepius, or that it may have been for putting patients in, as a form of shock-treatment. I don't know whether the statement tells more about guides or about ancient therapy itself, but at least it shows there is room for speculation.

We left Epidaurus at five and drove north, past Nauplion and Mycenae again, to Corinth, a trip of more than an hour. We were all tired and sticky when we got there, and besides the one-day tourists had already been over the place, on the way down, so the guide didn't spend much time on it. Ancient Corinth was a commercial center, preeminently, exploiting the trade across its isthmus. It also had a temple of Venus on the heights above it, and I have heard another guide make much of the prostitutes who held forth there. This one dwelt on less sensational things. "Corinth had the most emancipated society in Greece," she said. "It was a center for merchants and philosophers. Its people didn't like to fight. They were pacifists. They much preferred to pray to Venus."

That old Corinth was wiped out by the Romans in 146 B.C.; then later, in 44 B.C., a new city was built there by order of Julius Caesar. The new one seems to have followed the old one's spirit in stressing commerce, cosmopolitanism, and licence; and partly for this reason Saint Paul paid much attention to it when spreading Christianity to Europe. The link with Saint Paul undoubtedly is — or was — a main drawing-card of Corinth for Westerners. Much of the Roman forum area has been excavated by the American School of Classical Studies — our archaeological outfit in Greece — and the School may work on other parts of the ruins, at this level, in the future. In 1960, though, the School was digging in a shallower, Byzantine layer to the forum's side. In the past these Byzantine layers were often thrown away by archaeologists who were keen to get down to classical pay-dirt, but the modern theory, shared by the American School's director, Henry Robinson, holds that all layers should be studied carefully before they are discarded.

This latter information did not come from the guide that day. She merely took us quickly through the forum in the sunset hour, showing us a few outstanding points of interest, including a Doric temple of Apollo that the Romans had failed to smash. Then she led us back to the modern world, where a festive evening had begun. It was the Feast Day of Saints Peter and Paul or of the Twelve Apostles, I can't remember which. Crowds were thickening in the streets and cafés outside the ruins' enclosure. Whole pigs were being roasted on spits, here and there, over charcoal. I slipped into a café myself, had two quick *ouzos* to renew my strength, then found the bus and boarded it. Soon we were moving through the late June daylight, then through the dusk, and then the dark — when we got to Athens the night was under way there.

Perhaps I should mention here my second trip around that circuit, though I didn't make it till late September. Dicky and John Belmont had left by then, but I had been joined briefly by a lady cousin, and we took a five- or six-day tour by private car — a new experience for me in Greece. Motoring is a booming activity there now, thanks to the tourist fever. A few years ago the Greek road system was incredibly primitive by American or West European standards, but now it is being modernized in all directions. One can also bring one's car more easily to Greece now, for in the summer of 1960 a ferry service was opened from Brindisi.

An early touch of fall came just before we made this trip, with showers bringing clouds and coolness. We set out for Delphi at lunchtime one day, and in the mountains en route we found that hundreds or thousands of beehives had been moved in, to take advantage of some autumn flowering — perhaps of heather. We passed the hives beside the road from time to time — rectangular ones, laid out in rigid order, like rows of houses.

Delphi was beautiful, as always. We stayed there overnight, then crossed the Gulf of Corinth by ferry the next afternoon. The second night we spent at Patras, an uninspiring (to me) provincial town, then continued around the Peloponnesus's northwest corner and reached Olympia in the afternoon.

Along the road we passed a gypsy band. There are many gypsies in Greece, and one often comes on their camps or sees them walking in the villages. The camps have tall, polygonal — almost conical — tents that are nearly white, plus — as a rule — a lot of bright-colored bedding and rugs spread out to air. There are also carts, and donkeys, horses, and other animals around. This moving train we met had lots of animals too. People were riding on horse-drawn carts or on donkeys. They were leading dogs and goats, and carrying chickens and turkeys, and they had the carts piled high with their ragged, colorful gear. They were strung out for half a mile or more — men, women, and children, most of them dark, the women in long, outlandish dresses.

At Olympia we stopped only briefly, then we pushed eastward in the later afternoon and spent the night at Vitina, a village in the Arcadian mountains. There is an outfit in Greece called the Royal National Foundation, which does peasant uplift among other things, and this has lined up rooms, for tourists, in private homes in a score of Greek villages. Vitina is one of them, and we discovered a Foundation house there after a certain amount of inquiry. It had a Foundation label pasted on its door, though otherwise it seemed much like the village homes all over Greece where one may get rooms without institutional help. The family was pleasant, anyway — a sturdy, up-and-coming, rather pushy lot, whose children were sternly doing homework. My cousin and I went to a *taverna* for dinner, then came back and had a good night's sleep in rooms from which various children had been dislodged. The next morning we had breakfast there of tea, bread, and honey; and the whole stay cost less than a dollar apiece.

We set out early in the morning, and about nine o'clock we reached Tripolis, the main town of Arcadia, where we had coffee. Then we left the main tourist route — we doubled back to visit a famous old temple at Bassae, in the mountains to our southwest. The road to Bassae was a dirt one, very bumpy (though it is now being surfaced), and we crawled along it for a couple of hours. The scene was lonely, and once we passed a stark, forbidding medieval fortress on a hill. The people we met were solitary or only in pairs, off by themselves on the hillsides — gathering wood with a donkey, perhaps, or burning charcoal, or herding sheep with a dog — the sheep-dogs barked and chased our car.

The temple of Bassae was alone in the wild hills. It was of gray limestone, like the hills themselves, and it harmonized with them beautifully. It was in good repair comparatively, with nearly all its columns standing, and it had a special nobility in the stark and windswept scene. A few pink autumn crocuses were growing near it, and sheep bells were tinkling. The place had a caretaker, still in residence — at the end of the season — in a little house nearby, and we went and talked with him and bought some postcards. He seemed delighted to see visitors.

That afternoon — still detouring from the main route — we made our way down to Sparta, crossing the Taygetus mountains toward the end of the trip — they were green, steep, spacious, and cut by mighty gorges — a fit accompaniment to the old Spartan character. In Sparta itself we didn't get much feel of the ancient people — though we saw the fertile plain on which their rigid society existed — but on a little peak nearby, called Mistra, we visited some interesting Byzantine remains. Under medieval conditions Mistra was an almost impregnable height, and a fragment of the Byzantine Empire survived there through the twilight years — even after the fall of Constantinople. The height was densely populated, and a good deal is left of the old streets and buildings, especially the churches. There are three churches with good frescoes in them, some of which show an Italian Renaissance influence that was coming into Greece then and undermining, apparently, the last vestiges of Byzantine self-confidence. The frescoes in one church depict such unheard-of things — for Byzantine religious art — as secular scenes, bright-colored coffins, and even donkeys. A guide at Mistra told me, too, that the Mistra court had been a great center, in its closing period, of humanist philosophy. So as one stands there one can feel the moment when Byzantine civilization was fading out and the modern West beginning.

From Sparta we drove northeast — partly on a new road then being built — to the region of Mycenae and Epidaurus. In June I had seen the antiquities in those places, but I was glad to see them again and glad, of course, to show them off. So we had a good look at them, then spent a quiet night at Mycenae, and drove the next morning back to Athens.

IV

MYKONOS

Mykonos is one brown island in the blue Aegean — black-ish-brown, in many places, from stone outcrops. In summer its vegetation is arid. Its roads are of dun sand. Its hills are craggy, and stonewalls are everywhere. Yet despite this mineral quality its landscape is friendly and well peopled. Little white houses, often with fig trees near them, are dotted over it. On the roads you meet islanders again and again, walking or riding donkeys (the women ride side-saddle and wear sunbonnets). The island is not big — you can cross it on foot in three hours. It has an interior village, Ano Mera, and a seaport town and capital named Mykonos itself, which is a composition of white houses and narrow, twisting alleys. In this town too you meet local people, and also — in summer — throngs of foreigners, since Mykonos is the favorite Greek island of vacationers. It is favored especially by the French and Scandinavians, perhaps — aside from the Greeks themselves — but each week hundreds of Americans, British, and other Europeans swirl on and off it, too.

In the summer of 1960 I spent a month on Mykonos with Dicky and John Belmont — living in rooms belonging to

Apostolos Kousathanas, a seaman who runs the caïque, or
small-boat, service to the nearby classical shrine of Delos.
We had two rooms in an upstairs flat — it was really the
dower-house of the Kousathanas daughter, Maria, but she
was still unwed, and it was being used for lodgers. The flat
had one other room, and during the month we were there,
from early July to early August, this was occupied by a
series of Americans, Belgians, Swedes, and Athenians, usually in couples but sometimes in other combinations. In
décor the place was simple — indigenous — but graceful,
and it was cool and very clean. For our two rooms and the
use of a common bath, plus all our laundry and my break-
fasts — the boys went out for theirs — we paid five dollars a day. John Belmont is a student of archaeology, and
he often spent his mornings roaming through the landscape. Otherwise we all stayed in, reading or writing, till
one o'clock, when we moved off to the waterfront.

We lived in the center of town, and the water was a few
minutes away, along flagstoned alleys between shops and
whitewashed walls. The trip would take us northward, and
as we drew near the water itself we would begin to feel the
meltemi, the cool north wind of summertime. It didn't
pierce deep into the alleys themselves, but on the waterfront, which faces north, it bore with all its strength. On
very windy days we would have to struggle through the
last few yards of whichever alley we were traveling. Then
we would burst out; the water ahead would be covered
with whitecaps; and we could be sure that we would lunch
indoors that day. In calmer weather we could lunch on the
flagstones of the esplanade, before one of three *tavernas*
that did business there; these would have their chairs and
tables out already, under awnings. We would take a table,
then go to the kitchen and order our food from the stove,

in the Greek *taverna* style. Usually I had *moussaka* with
bread, wine, and a salad of tomatoes. The boys would have
the same, or something near it, and the meal would cost a
dollar and a half for all.

We would sit there talking, eating, and looking around.
The tourists on the move then might be few. Of those in
residence, some would be at the beaches still, and some
would be coming back from Delos — the caïques, which
left for that island at nine in the morning and began the return at one, took half an hour, an hour, or even longer, depending on the wind. As for new tourists, they would seldom have arrived yet — the little liners from the Piraeus
did not come till late in the day, as a rule, and the cruise
boats, which flooded Mykonos with visitors on Fridays,
did not put in till early afternoon. There would be enough
people to take up the *taverna* tables, and some of the café
tables around about; but the rest of the esplanade — some
twenty yards wide from shops to water — would be an
open glare. This band curved gracefully in a semicircle, one
end running out, as a jetty, into the sea, and the other join-
ing the bulk of land eventually (the town itself was on a
promontory). The curving row of shops and restaurants —
the buildings sparkling white — were on the esplanade's
south side, the water on its north. The water was shallow
near the restaurants — the Mykonos harbor is not deep —
and there was a foreshore there, unpaved, where boats were
beached. Others would be anchored farther out, or tied up
to the jetty.

We wouldn't linger over lunch, but would rise and go
to our afternoon pursuits — usually walking to some fairly
distant beach, swimming and napping there, and walking
back again. Mykonos port, though facing north, is on the
island's west side; and a long ridge, running north to south,

stands between it and the interior.* If we came back over this late enough, the sea would gleam before us in the low sun, and the white town below would look like phosphorus. We would go home, take a shower perhaps, call on friends or rustle our books and papers, and return one by one to the waterfront toward dinner time. The shadows would be creeping over the flagstones then, and they would be dramatic. The Greek tourists on the island — vacationers from Athens, mainly — would be promenading, as is their custom. Droves of them would be walking back and forth along the curve, chatting with their side-mates and nodding to those they passed. The foreign tourists, unless bent on errands, would often be sedentary at the café tables.

I usually reached the waterfront, by myself, around eight, expecting a rendezvous with the boys. If I got there first I would sit at a table and demand an *ouzo*, which would come eventually — slowly, for all the cafés were crowded. With it would be a tiny saucer of *mezedes* or Greek hors d'oeuvres — perhaps a couple of ripe olives, perhaps a slice or two of cucumber or tomato, perhaps some diced octopus with a sliver of cheese or fragment of a sausage. Sometimes, too, there would be a piece of bread, no bigger than a domino. One part of the midget ensemble would have a toothpick stuck in it, and the whole would be composed with the greatest care, like a Japanese flower arrangement. I would sit there, sipping and nibbling, and watching the red-and-green sunset band to my west. Then soon the boys, and perhaps some friends, would join me, and we would have more *ouzos*, then go to eat.

Early in our stay we dined at the same *tavernas*, by and large, as we lunched at, but later we found one in an alley, ten or twenty yards back from the waterfront, that was still

---

* More properly, the ridge is the edge of a plateau that makes up the town's hinterland.

more to our liking. It was run by another member of
the Kousathanas family — huge on Mykonos — who was
known as Piperia, or Pepper, because of a tendency to put
too much pepper in the food. He was a slight, solemn, hard-
working man, with only one teen-age son to help him run
the place. He had long since curbed the pepper tendency,
but he was not ashamed of its reputation, and he had a big
sign over his door saying "PIPERIA," by which name the
place was known. It was actually a wine-shop, rather than
a *taverna*. At midday it sold almost no food at all, and in
the evening it concentrated on one main dish. If there had
been a good catch of fish that day — of mackerel or red
mullet — the customers got that. Otherwise they got tasty
meatballs of Piperia's mixing. In addition one could have
excellent bread and salad — and wine, of course — and
Piperia's son would go out and buy a melon if one wished.

The wine was stored in big casks, mounted atop man-
high wooden frameworks in the back room — against the
walls there — and most of the tables were located under
these. The place was warmly lit; it was small; it had a musician in it now and then; and it was patronized mainly by the
fishermen and other waterfront characters of the island. A
few tourists came to it, but they were not many, and seldom
were they newcomers, for the place was hard to find, and
once found was rather puzzling — its ways were not immediately plain, that is, and Piperia spoke no foreign tongue.

The tourists who did come fell in with the spirit of the
place and didn't change it much. This was true of Mykonos
as a whole, indeed, so far as I could tell. Many foreign
purists in Greece — and Greeks as well — complain that
Mykonos has been ruined by the tourists, yet I never felt
that. They swarmed there — almost, at times, as crowds
swarm in Grand Central Station — yet the island seemed to
absorb them. It had a defense in depth. The whole mad

rush milled about on the waterfront — with its shops, *ta-vernas*, and cafés — and many tourists, I imagine, never got farther than that. Others penetrated to the inner alleys, in driblets, and they were sopped up there somehow. Those who stayed in town for long would be transformed. Most Mykoniats let out rooms, and I believe there were hundreds — even thousands — of foreigners staying in these at times, but they seemed to get Mykonized somehow and not be obtrusive. As for the rest of the island, few tourists went beyond the two nearest beaches, the fashionable ones. Almost no one got into the real interior, which went its way unchanged.

After dinner one could have coffee or a drink on the waterfront, or one could promenade there. If the *meltemi* was strong, the waves would be leaping up blackly, with bright lights reflected on them. The esplanade would be crowded, and if an inter-island boat — a small liner — was coming or going the people would be thickest near the jetty. Lots of Mykoniats would be there along with the outlanders — the women watching quietly, as at a movie, and the men busying around to carry baggage or find roomers. The harbor was so shallow that the liners couldn't tie up there, as they do at many islands.* They anchored outside, and the passengers came ashore in launches — launch after launch of them in the peak evenings.

The biggest landing operation, though, was that on Friday afternoons, when two or three cruise boats — the

* In 1961 a new deep-water jetty was finished at Mykonos, and now most liners do tie up there — they *pleurizein*, in the Greek phrase — i.e., they "pleurize" or bring their ribs alongside. This changes the style of travel a good deal, and other things are changing it too. For instance a big, fast new boat, the *Delos*, came into the Aegean trade in 1961, serving as a cruise boat and a liner as well. It cuts down the travel time to Mykonos and other islands, and it makes Wet Greece seem smaller.

Semiramis, the *Aigion,* and perhaps the *Kriti* — would appear outside the harbor. They would be finishing a five-day conducted tour of the Aegean, and at Mykonos they would let their passengers ashore — several hundred of them — to spend the afternoon and evening as they chose, before returning to the Piraeus in the night. They would start coming ashore right after our lunchtime — an endless chain of launches bringing them, discharging them, and hurrying back. Each launch would have two dozen passengers, more or less, packed in and sitting meek and mild. There would be old women, pretty girls in bright dresses, and men in shirts and shorts — most carrying bathing-suits, many carrying cameras, and some even suitcases, with a view to staying awhile. On the jetty they would be met by little boys with handbills advertising — in Greek, French, and English — an outdoor restaurant on the town's south edge. The English version of these read as follows:

DANCING RESTAURANT GREEN
GARDEN "FABRICA"

LADIES AND GENTLEMEN.

During your stay in the wonderful and sunshine Mykonos. You are invited just five minutes away from the site of Megali ammos beach.

Where you may into a nice and attractive environment and with unmagined lowest, prices to taste the famous Greek Kitchen. Serving you meals and all kind drinks on which time will entertain you a famous Athenian jazz band orchestra which entertainment will last until very morning.

NOTE: The Restaurant serves at noon time meal and drinks. at usual Restaurant prices, under garden's tree dewiness.

This charming picture would not appeal to the tourists at that moment, for they would have just been fed on their boats. Most of them would be heading for a beach, and after that for shopping. The merchants would be ready for them, on the waterfront and back in the town itself. There were many regular shops along the esplanade, and on Fridays there were many hawkers, too, with stalls. These would have their wares out — sandals, espadrilles, shirts, sweaters, knitted jackets, skirts, scarves, bags, gourds, sponges, conches, dresses, straw hats, cloth hats, tam o'shanters, bedspreads — even dolls, ship-models, and toy windmills. The clothes and fabrics, especially, would be conspicuous, for Mykonos is a weaving center. They would be hung, in their bright colors, above the stalls and on the shopfronts, and the *meltemi* would make them flap and stir. The waves would beat on the jetty meanwhile; the sun would gleam on the white buildings; and the tourists would surge across the waterfront and disappear.

Toward evening they would be back again, greatly thickening the crowd. In their bright-colored cruising clothes — diverse, fantastic, and now enriched by Mykonos additions — they would seem, in the lamp-lit dusk, like a circus spectacle; one would half-wait for the band to strike up and the elephants to come padding on. Then after dinner they would get on their launches and depart. Their coming and going changed the island's population in quantity, and also a little bit in quality, for the cruise tourists seemed to be slightly richer and slightly less sophisticated than the long-term ones — less able to find their way around, that is, and more dependent on travel agencies and organization.

Among the long-run tourists, as has been said, the French and Scandinavians were prominent. Mykonos is well known in France, one gathers — in part, no doubt, because French archaeologists, working out of there, have done the excavations on Delos. The Scandinavians come to Greece because it is so different from their own land — they keep on coming, too, far into the sunny fall. Why they should concen-

trate on Mykonos I do not know, but my impression —
without statistics to back it up — is that they do so, very
much. Some German tourists come to the island, but not
many (it seems) in proportion to those elsewhere in Greece.
The richer Germans like more pretentious places, apparently, and the poorer avoid even the modest outlay that
Mykonos entails. Many German students come to Greece
in the summer with knapsacks and supplies of food. They
hike, sleep out of doors, and have a healthy time of it for
next to nothing. A favorite place of theirs is Mount Athos,
a peninsula studded with Orthodox monasteries, where they
can walk about and take advantage of monastic hospitality
— a five-day limit was recently put on foreigners' visits to
Mount Athos, and one hears that this was mainly a defense
against these guests.

A number of British visitors come to Mykonos, too, of
course, but not enough to put their stamp on it deeply —
and the same goes for Belgians, Dutch, Swiss, Canadians,
and so on. Americans come in great numbers — especially
on the cruise boats — and they do Americanize the place
somewhat. I have heard the cry of "Hiya, cowboy!" on
the waterfront. One also finds much indirect American influence there. I remember especially, on the jetty, a French
male tourist in a pair of French-made blue-jeans. They had
zippers across both hip pockets, which Dicky and John
Belmont thought very strange. A few American beatniks
are to be seen on the island, wearing their rigid uniform —
they and the Mykoniat fishermen are the only ones who
walk barefoot on the esplanade. There are many other
youthful visitors, too, and that is one of the nice things
about Mykonos. Students from all nations come there, lead
a healthy life, and mob around together, conversing seri-
ously.

Many Greeks come to the island — Athenians of large or
modest means. Some have summer houses there, on the ridge
above the town. They are different from most of the local
people — more *chic*, more city-slicker — and are looked on
pretty much as foreigners. I heard one Athenian complain
that summer, in fact, that the Mykoniats spoke to him in
English. Now and then some of the richest men in Greece
— the real big-bourgeois, in the Onassis-Niarchos class —
come in on yachts, which may tie up at the jetty for a day
or two. The yachts of such people, like their merchant
ships, are apt to fly the Liberian or Panamanian flag, which
is a device for evading their country's regulations, but is not,
apparently, resented by other Greeks. Two or three times
that summer I saw a handsome blue yacht at the jetty with
the Liberian flag on it — this is like our own, but with one
star instead of fifty. I remarked on it to a Greek acquaint-
ance, and he nodded. "Yes," he answered matter-of-factly.
"If a boat in these waters has the Liberian flag that means
it's Greek."

Not all the fashionable people on Mykonos are outsiders,
of course. There are rich old families on the island whose
members know Athens, and perhaps western Europe, well.
These have their own relations with the outside world, and
with few exceptions they keep clear of the Northern in-
vaders.

Northerners have been drawn to the Mediterranean since
the dawn of history. In ancient times they came as barbarian
attackers. In the Middle Ages they came as "Crusaders,"
Viking seamen, or adventurers about to join the Varangian
guard of the Byzantine emperor. They couldn't stay away,
and now they come as tourists. They bring money into
Greece, and in return they get unwonted things like wine,

sunshine, and a non-puritan environment. The Greeks are used to them — to their slowness, introversion, hard drinking, and other non-Hellenic ways. Greeks can talk and think faster than almost any Northerner, and one gets the impression that they are rather amused by us, though they politely conceal this from all but other Greeks. The amusement need not hurt the Northerners especially. That spring on Mount Athos a Greek monk had told me how he and his fellows had made fun, during the war, of some Germans stationed on the coast there, to spy on shipping. "They loved to drink," he said. "We used to give them lots of *raki,* and they would get drunk, and we would watch them and laugh to ourselves." I listened to the monk attentively, yet I suspected that the Germans had enjoyed the game at least as much as he had.

The Northern tourists, most of whom come to Greece for brief excursions, have less chance to study the natives than vice versa. But I know one Norwegian who has lived on Mykonos for some time, and he has begun developing theories. He finds his neighbors very sane, for one thing, by Northern standards. "I don't know what mental problems these extroverted Greeks can have," he said to me during the summer, "unless it's going out and getting lost in space." He fell silent for a while. "They are all hysterics," he went on. "A Greek would have to be treated for extreme phlegmaticness if he weren't hysterical." Then he fell silent again. Northerners are always falling silent.

The North-South differences are as interesting, perhaps, as those between Orient and Occident, and Mykonos is one of the world's best spots to watch them in. The Northerners wander blissfully on the waterfront — sun-battered, with burned and drawn faces, and bleached and stringy hair. The Greeks smile cordially to them, but keep within the shade.

The coarse brown sand on Mykonos gives the island good beaches, here and there, on all its coasts. The ones we went to most often were about an hour's walk away. We would leave the port after lunch and climb the hinterland plateau. Once there we would proceed either by a sandy road, wide enough for an auto — Mykonos has a dozen motor vehicles now, including taxis, trucks, and motorcycles — or by one of countless narrow lanes, between stone walls, that run about the landscape. The island is so endowed with rocks that their disposal is a problem, and for untold ages they have been stacked up in walls with these lanes between them; the lanes are often paved with rocks, too — sometimes with bare expanses of the living rock, sometimes with steps built in. They take a lot of knowing, for they wander unpredictably, and the walls are often too high for one to look over (they are also flimsy — very thin — and hard to climb without pulling down). A lane that seems to head north will eventually take you west, and so on. Yet the trip is always pleasant, wherever it goes; and in a month's time you can memorize the routes you want to use.

Besides turning, the lanes struggle up and down little hills. The Aegean islands are continuations, by and large, of the mountain ranges in Dry Greece, but their relief — that of Mykonos especially — seems to be less sharp. Interior Mykonos looks a good deal like the Tibetan Plateau — sepia-colored, bare, bright-lit, and rolling, though often punctuated by smallish crags. It has a Tibetan peacefulness, too, and simplicity. Aside from the steady, cool north wind there is little agitation on it, and the people go about their business in a slow, time-tested way. When we first went to Mykonos, in early July, they were still threshing the spring harvest. They did this on round stone floors, placed out in the fields. They laid the wheat out on the floors, to the depth of a foot

or two, then drove animals around and around on it to dash
the grain off. They used a strange mélange of animals —
cows, mules, and donkeys indiscriminately — to do this job.

Other animals one met on the island — aside from cats,
which were plentiful in the town — included dogs, pigs,
sheep, and goats. The dogs would be at the farmhouses,
often ready to bark as one passed by. The pigs would not be
seen from afar as a rule; they would be near the houses, and
behind stone walls; yet I was told that nearly every Mykoniat family had one; and the island is famous for its sausages.
The sheep and goats would be in the little fields, surrounded
by the high stone walls, and the goats, at least, would often
be hobbled in addition. Sometimes children would be
watching the animals — children abounded in the countryside, peering over the walls or playing near the small, stone
whitewashed houses.

The fields themselves were dead-looking by the time we
got there — with dry dirt in them or old brown grass and
stubble.* More lively were the fig trees, the vineyards, the
melon patches, and the watered gardens, which grew fine
eggplants and tomatoes then. The figs and grapes came into
season while we were on the island; by custom, both are
supposed to be eaten on August first in Greece, and that
morning Mrs. Kousathanas brought us heaping plates of
them. The melons began in July, and they came from Delos
as well as Mykonos — both islands have good sandy soil.
Both grew little round watermelons (a North American
contribution, I think, in the last analysis), along with different kinds of what we call the Persian melon, the same
as are found in Central Asia, clear across to northwest China

* I later stayed on Mykonos in the winter, and it was very different
— stormy, rainy, gushy, and green. But the next summer it was brown
all over again.

— each oasis having its own variety. In Greece these melons are called *peponia* (watermelons are *karpouzia*), and on Mykonos they came in all shapes from round to almost needle-pointed. Inside they ranged from white to nearly red, and they were sweet and deliciously refreshing. They were never, to my knowledge, eaten with a spoon. When in the open people merely slashed them, with a knife, into new-moon slivers and ate these with their hands. In the more formal restaurants the melons came in moon-slices, too, for eating with a knife and fork, and at Piperia's the meat was cut into small pieces and served in one big dish, with forks supplied to everyone at the table. Salads and even fish at Piperia's were often eaten in the same communal way — it is, in fact, a strong custom in Greece, and it makes for conviviality there, as it does in China.

The melon patches were apt to be far from houses and subject to raiding by birds. One patch that we used to walk through had an old man with a shotgun hanging around it sometimes. The place was on sandy soil just inland from our favorite northern beach — we went through the melons, then over a rise of sand dunes, then down onto the beach itself, which stretched in a handsome crescent for hundreds of yards. It lay along a bay that faced exactly north — outside this the blue sea went unbroken to the horizon; and the *meltemi*, in sweeping down over that space, developed lots of force. There was always wind and motion on the water. On arriving we would change and swim awhile, then come out and sleep on the beach — I for an hour or so, the boys perhaps for less. Then we would take another dip, dress, and start for home. The beach was usually deserted, and it was peaceful to doze there, with the soft and rhythmic wave-beat in your ears. But if the *meltemi* was very strong, the sand would blow and sting us, and we learned on windy days to leave that beach alone and go to another, on the island's south side, that we knew. This had a high bluff behind it and was always calm. It had a stretch of rocky coast beside it, too, where we could swim with a mask and investigate the weeds and fishes — a continuation, under water, of the Mykonos landscape, with fantastic variations: lush greenery and sparkling fauna.

The south coast had three or four beaches, in fact, that we used to walk to, and one of these had two reed shanties where you could get refreshments. The first day I went there I happened to be alone. I came to the nearer shanty, which was the size of a one-car garage and had a peasant girl standing by it. She beckoned to me shyly, and we agreed that I would change my clothes in the place — it was bare except for a shelf, and a bench and table resting on the sand. I took a dip, came out and napped in the sun, took another dip, and finally returned to the shanty. No one was there; but some flowers, a bunch of grapes, a bottle of *ouzo*, and a pitcher of water had been laid out on the table. I made the most of this surprise, then on leaving I found the girl and gave her ten drachmas — a little over thirty cents — which seemed to please her a lot. After that I went back often, with or without the boys. We found that the hut belonged to a peasant family who lived just behind it amid some hedges and gardens; and later in our stay, on a Sunday, we got them to make lunch for us and two friends. This was served under a fig tree in the garden, with inadequate furniture and table-ware, but with much spirit. We had some chicken soup; the chicken itself; some eggs and sausages; a salad of tomatoes, cheese, and olives; and at the end some figs and grapes — all washed down by plenty of *retsina*. When sated, we moved back to the beach and beach-house, for swimming, napping, and more festivities through the afternoon. We gave the family a hundred drachmas that day ($3.33), and they tried hard to give us back some change.

Through all these scenes the *meltemi* kept on playing — through nearly all, that is, for we sometimes had a day or two of calm. These would be dead and listless, like the sinister spells of wind — *sirocco, khamsin, Föhn,* and so on — that afflict some other countries. I would go through my usual motions during them, but would feel, almost, that life had been suspended. Then the breeze would begin again, getting stronger and stronger. The water would come to life, and air would cool, and the island would be a paradise once more.

Mykonos is famous for its weaving, but its masonry, too, is a fine popular art. The raw materials are everywhere and the people use them naturally. They make good scarecrows out of rocks — building up statues and then clothing them — and they put their stonewalls down and up with great abandon. The walls are often thin and lacy, so that you can see the sky through them, and feel the breeze; and in line with this they are treated almost as plastic matter, rather than fixed institutions. The gateway to a field may be closed not by bars or a gate, but simply by more stone wall — if a man is putting animals in such a field, he merely tears this gap open, then fills it up again.

Walls are dismantled for other reasons, too. One evening the boys and I went with Greek friends and others to a *paneghyri,* or saint's-day festival, at a little church in the open country. We found dozens of people there — singing, dancing, and feasting in bright lamplight — and those not in motion were sitting on stools made from rocks. The food and drink were on tables made from rocks as well, and we found that all this material had come from a big wall near-by

— more of it came soon, indeed, to make some stools for us.

Subtlety gets into the simplest Mykoniat stonework. The lanes on the island often cross bare stretches of the living rock. This seems natural, and you walk along them thinking you are on pure Mother Earth. But soon you notice that steps have been cut in here and there. Then you see that other rocks have been added, to make more steps or fill in holes — though sometimes you can't be sure they didn't grow there. Then in time — without being able to say just when — you find yourself on full-rigged steps or flagstones. It is as if masonry were meant just to touch things up, and not to be a formal business as in other countries.

Often the Mykoniat stonewalls are elaborated, in that spirit, by the insertion of stiles. A stile can be made by putting a long stone in a wall so that its ends stick out on either side, making steps, and this is often done — or if the wall is high, two or three stones may be inserted, in echelon, making flights of steps. The stile is often mortared, for security — the wall as a whole being made dry. It can also be whitewashed for emphasis, and for spotting from afar. Whitewashing is, in fact, a main part of the mason's bag of tricks on Mykonos. Stone well-heads by the lanes —and the troughs beside them, for watering animals — are often whitewashed. Flagstones are whitewashed, too, but in a special way — usually the cracks alone, with an inch or two on either side of them, are whitened — the white is in a network, that is, with the central portions of the stones left bare, like holes. But the edges of an alley — the outside foot, or half a foot, adjoining the bottoms of the house walls — are often whitewashed solid. In this way whitewash comes to indicate domesticity, and around some houses it is deliberately used for that. These are ones built not on man-made foundations but on the big rock ledges that are common in the landscape, and the whitewash signifies — much as does a lawn or flower-garden — that those particular regions are civilized. Sometimes the areas even have networks whitewashed on them, as if pretending there are flagstones there.

Virtually all the houses in Mykonos town are whitewashed. This gives brilliant reflected light in the sunny daytime — it is like a snow-scene as you walk around.* The bright-lit alleys are narrow — so narrow that you are in trouble if you meet a mule or donkey there with panniers. They also twist bewilderingly; and there were parts of the town that I never, in my whole month's stay, could figure out. All this crookedness baffles the wind, which may be a reason for its prevalence — the inner streets are calm on the wildest day. I have also heard that the baffling of pirates, who used to be common in the Aegean, was an aim of the layout. If so, the purpose must have been achieved — a stranger rushing into town would soon find himself going in circles or running forever into dead ends, these cunningly overlooked from the rooftops. At times the streets are almost like practical jokes — certain through-streets are made to seem like dead ends, as you look down them; and one alley gets so narrow, as it goes along, that you must turn sideways to pass through it.

Many Mykonos houses have separate flats, with outer stairways, for their upper story. I have heard that this results from the Greek marriage system — that originally the houses had only one story, but that the owners later built the upper flats for their daughters' dowries. This was exactly the function, anyway, of the flat we lived in — it had come to Apostolos Kousathanas with his wife; and in time,

* James Burke, the *Life* photographer, reports that his light-meter reading on the Mykonos waterfront is the highest he has known — higher even than those in the Arabian desert.

presumably, it would leave him with his daughter. I don't
know when it was built, but it was a delightful place. A
flight of stone steps led up from the street to a little entry
terrace in front of it. The steps' vertical surfaces were
whitewashed, and its horizontal ones — the treads — were
of bare pale marble. The stairway was irregular in design,
and seemed — like much of the island's masonry — to war-
rant the name of sculpture. The flat had another terrace at
its back, too, where a bathroom had recently been installed.
There were some marble slabs in the threshhold leading to
this terrace, and one of them was an old carved relief —
Byzantine, I suppose — of flowers, which the builders must
have found somewhere. The rooms and hall inside were
plastered, high-ceilinged, and cool. I lived in what was
originally the kitchen, on the north end, and some of the
basic fittings were still there. Under the window was a sink
that had been hewn from a single piece of marble. Its surfaces were roughly plane on the top and inside, but the
underneath had been left more rugged — hardly dressed at
all. The sink was a rich off-white in color, and pleasant to
the touch; and to have it there was like having a statue in
the room. The stove was a dainty little creation of brown
tiles, set waist high in a wall, atop another big thick slab
of marble. The room's floor was of tiles, too — black-and-
white checkered, cool and smooth. The plaster walls were
whitewashed, with a blue tone, and the wooden trim was
cream colored. The boys' room — normally the bedroom
anyway — was more elegant still. The flat was not at all
grand — just part of a fisherman's dowry — but it was done
with an exquisite taste that I related to the Mykoniat genius
for stonework.

Much could be written about the more formal architecture of Mykonos. There are over three hundred and

fifty small churches on the island, though the population is only four thousand. Many of these are votive offerings — thanks for being saved from a shipwreck or other danger. Only a few are used for services. The bulk of them are associated with particular families, and many have tombs in them; the bones of dead Mykoniats are often disinterred after three years and entombed, permanently, in the family church walls. A few of the churches have elaborate icons and carvings, and even original over-all designs, but most are simple little whitewashed affairs, with vaulted red roofs, that dot the landscape along with the simple houses. (One of them, the so-called Church of the Cat, is no bigger than a dog kennel — it was built by a sailor, I have heard, who made a vow of a church when shipwrecked near Gibraltar, but who used up nearly all his money while getting back from there.)

Flat stones, buil: up together almost like card-houses, and then whitewashed, are used to embellish some of the Mykonos chimney pots, and they are also used, with great inventiveness, to adorn the tops of big stone dovecotes that abound on the island. These structures, the story goes, were made in older times for carrier pigeons, which the Mykoniat sea-captains would take on their ships for sending messages home. They are as big, sometimes, as the island's smaller houses, and in form they resemble the square type of Gothic tower — the one with four pinnacles arising from its corners. On some dovecotes these pinnacles, and the whole upper structures, are done with flat stones put together in lace-like wedding-cake fantasy, and they add a lot to the island's masonic charm.

These frills aside, the virtue of the Mykoniat architecture lies in its simple, solid, cubistic, Pueblo-Indian, white-surfaced masses. The architecture on Mykonos and some of the

other Cyclades was much studied by Le Corbusier between
the two wars, and through him it has had much influence on
modern design. Besides being closely related to the Mykonos
landscape, therefore, it is related to the modern Western
style, which may help explain why visitors are so much at
home with it. Good modern buildings, in turn, should come
naturally to Mykonos in its present vogue. Some visitors
have, in fact, recently built houses, on the heights above the
town, that try to combine a Mykoniat appearance with
modern luxury. These are not, so far, especially distin-
guished. The most interesting work in that line (I think)
is a new tourist hotel that was opened that summer in the
town's south fringes, overlooking the sea. It consists of
several rectangular two-story blocks made of Mykonos
stone, unwhitewashed, but with broad white-painted bands
— smart and gleaming — around the buildings' tops. These
bands suggest the glisten of the town; the natural stone
suggests the island; and in scale and shape the blocks go
well with the cubistic architecture around them. I don't
know what the inside of that hotel is like — it opened just
as I left — but its outside seems a case of good modern
design, and it certainly fits its background. It is a happy
offshoot of the tourist boom.

The origins of this Mykoniat architecture are dim, but
they must go far back. The island was probably inhabited
four thousand years ago — John Belmont, in his searches,
found remains of Bronze- or Stone-Age settlements on it.
There are few references to Mykonos in classical times, and
presumably it was not important then. But Delos, only a
couple of miles away, was very important, and thickly
settled; and in the remains there, which we visited several
times, one can see many foreshadowings of Mykonos. This

is true especially of a Roman-sponsored city that flourished
on Delos around the second century B.C. Much of it has
been uncovered by the French archaeologists, and one can
see that its inhabitants built good stone houses on the Mykonos scale. The city's streets were the size of the present
Mykonos alleys, too, and the shops were like the smaller
Mykonos shops, with living quarters attached. Then many
Delian buildings had cisterns under them, as buildings do
now on Mykonos (for water is scarce on both islands), and
the round stone cistern-heads — with grooves worn in
them by ropes — look about the same in both places. There
was a rope-grooved cistern-head on our back upper terrace,
through which Mrs. Kousathanas and Maria used to haul up
water for the bathroom, and I think it would have seemed
quite familiar to a Roman Delian.

That Roman city was prodigious. It had over a hundred
thousand inhabitants, and it covered much of the island,
which is only three miles long. It flourished for a century
or two, being promoted by the Romans as a rival to Rhodes,
which they did not favor. They made it a free port, and it
became an entrepôt in the East Mediterranean trade —
goods being transshipped there between Asia and Greece
and Rome. Huge amounts of grain and slaves, especially,
were dealt in; and a rich international populace lived there
— a wealth of jewelry and other luxury goods has been
turned up in the excavations. Temples of Syrian and Egyptian gods were built, and the tiny spot of land became a
center of cultural interchange (the temple of the Egyptian
god Serapis was built beside a little ravine called the Inopus
River, which was supposed, in mythology, to be a continuation of the Nile — the lizards on Delos were supposed to
be Nile crocodiles, which had shrunk in their long, con-
stricted trip from home).

This Roman-period boom was not Delos's first time as a world center. As the supposed birthplace of Apollo, it was earlier the religious, cultural, and political hub of the Aegean civilization, and it was important in the shift of that civilization's leadership to Athens in the fifth century B.C. From prehistoric times it was one of the greatest shrines in the Greek world. It had such prestige that delegations from rival islands could get together on it and discuss their problems in an atmosphere of religious truce — the nearest equivalent, then, to our atmosphere of international law. From this background the Delian League, an early attempt at a United Nations, developed.* At first, in the seventh and sixth centuries, the Delian association was an island affair, led much of the time by Naxos, a large member of the Cyclades lying to the southeast. Then in the fifth century the Athenians came to dominate it, Pericles eventually removing the Delian League's rich treasury to Athens itself, and investing it in his building program on the Acropolis. After that Delos became less important — until the Roman boom — though it still had many gifts and ceremonies lavished on it.

The Roman flowering ended, essentially, in 86 B.C., when the island was sacked by the Asiatic invader Mithradates. The place has been in decline ever since, and now there are only a few small houses on it, plus the ruins, a museum, and a tourist pavilion. The ruins are said to be the most extensive in Greece. Those of the earlier flowering — the Apollo sanctuary — are on a big level space near the sea. There are acres of remains there, including a few fine pieces of archaic sculpture — a row of guardian lions, especially, and the

---

* Guides and others liken both the Delian League and the Amphictyonic League at Delphi to early UNs and in both cases they seem justified.

torso of a vast Apollo statue erected by the Naxians — this last is of rough-surfaced marble, warm and creamy in the sunlight, and it stands up before the blue sea.

The Roman city — the excavated part — lies near the sanctuary on a hillside; and this in turn leads up to a little peak, 368 feet high, which dominates the island and which in very ancient times had shrines of Zeus and Athena on it. From it one gets a splendid view in all directions. Round about lie various of the honey-colored Cyclades — Syra, Tinos, Mykonos, Naxos, Paros, and a very near one called Reneia or Big Delos. Short of these, on a calm day, one can look right down into the sea and distinguish the different kinds of bottom there — sand, rocks, or seaweed — in various colors of clear blue. On windy days the scene is more exciting. There is a strait between Delos and Reneia, and the driven water comes through this like rapids — roaring and dashing on the rocks. Then on the shore is the rippling brown grass, mixed with poppies, thistles, and other weeds; and inside this are the pale gray ruins — the forest of old columns — of the sanctuary.

I usually went to Delos on my Sunday mornings. The caïques went there sometimes in the afternoons, by special arrangement, but they preferred the mornings because the *meltemi* would be lighter then. Yet even coming back at midday — against the wind — could be hard at times. Then the boats would toss about, and follow a crooked course in the lee of shores; and the passengers who stayed on deck would be drenched with spray. Usually there were two caïques in the fleet, though there could be more — Apostolos Kousathanas, our landlord, seemed to be the over-all admiral and business manager of the operation, rather than the skipper of any particular boat.

The boat I usually traveled on, the *Margarita*, had a big friendly captain, and his pretty daughter was his engineer. One could look down the hatch of the little engine-room and see her bending over the pistons. She had long glistening black tresses and a curvesome body clad in a rough blue shirt and denim slacks. Her feet were bare and her toenails painted, and an occasional black oil spot on her feet would go with these delightfully. In idle moments she might come on deck and play maternally with some passenger's child. But when the going got rough she would be down below again, her tender hand on the throttle.

The Mykoniats were friendly, even by Greek standards, and they always had a good word when you met them. In the morning in Greece one may say *kal'imera* — "good day" — and later on *kal'espera* — "good evening." In between these, or at any time — and whether on meeting or parting — one may say *chairete* — "be happy" — or even *chaire*, which is "be happy" in the familiar singular. In a more boisterous mood one may say *yiasu!* — "good health" — or *yiahara!* — "health and happiness." And then one may say *adio* for good-by. Mykoniat women, I found, leaned toward *chairete*, and I usually said that to them myself. Men riding on donkeys were apt to say *yiasu!*, and I often said it to them in anticipation, but then they might say something else.

Different islands seem to have different usages. On Samos, where I walked a good deal earlier in the summer, nearly everyone — of whatever class — seemed to say *yiasu!*, heartily, and on Rhodes, where I walked later on, they seemed to prefer *kal'imera*. The great Mykoniat peculiarity was to say *adio* on meeting as well as on parting — I suppose they got this from the analogy of *chairete*. Whatever they said, anyway, they said it with *bonhomie*, and it made the pleasant sandy roads still pleasanter.

Several Mykoniats spoke English, and of this number some were retired first-generation Greek-Americans, who had been in the States long enough to have green passports and social-security pensions — our social-security checks can make a man a prince on a Greek island. The spot in the United States where most of these Mykoniats had lived was Joliet, Illinois — I suppose one of them had gone there early in the game and had been followed by a train of friends and relatives. I remember Joliet, from boyhood newspapers, as the site of the Illinois state prison, where the Chicago gangsters would be put, yet to Mykonos it was the very heart of the New World. New York was well known, too, several Mykoniats having been there as merchant seamen. These people with experience of America like to talk about it, and did so enthusiastically.

When you got to know the Mykoniats, they would offer you a glass of wine, in Piperia's, or a piece of melon as you were walking. They were hospitable. At the evening *paneghyri* that I have mentioned, they gave us wine and fruit and also sprigs of basil to smell — the Greeks love aromatic herbs, and they pass them around at parties like refreshments. That was on the eve of Saint Panteleimon's day. We walked to the festival by dark with our Greek friends, taking perhaps an hour on a road and then a winding lane — going by feel and starlight. The people danced circular Greek dances that night — swaying, skipping, and leaping — with steps and music that seemed Asiatic to my untutored senses. There was a second *paneghyri* of Saint Panteleimon, too, held the next day at a big house in the island's interior, which had once been a monastery and had

a richly decorated old church inside it. The boys and I
stopped there on the way back from swimming. The house
was three stories high and had a terrace and battlements at
the top, like a fortress. It had a central courtyard onto which
the church opened, and this was crowded with festive people when we got there. Two or three pairs of musicians
were playing, in turn, and two groups of islanders were
dancing expertly. Men were selling *ouzo* and soft drinks at
a couple of improvised bars. The church, a small one, was
all decked out, and people were jammed inside it, as in the
courtyard — moving slowly through the rituals of worship
and merry-making. After half an hour we walked on back
to Mykonos town, and along the way we kept meeting
people, all dressed up, still going to the festival — I suppose
it lasted far into the evening.

The musicians at these feasts seemed mostly to be amateur. One lived near our lodgings, and we used to hear him
and got to know him a little. His name was Michaelis, and
he was a builder by trade — reputed to be the best on the
island. Every evening after work he would come home and
start immediately — without even getting the plaster off
him — to play a bagpipe, while his teen-age son beat a drum
to accompany him. We would hear him across the back
yards, and in time we took to dropping in on him. He was a
fine-looking man, with wide, strong hands, a wide, strong,
craggy face, and a dome of a head above it. His bagpipe
was made from a simple goatskin, its openings all stitched up
except for the front legs, one of which held a mouthpiece
and the other a short bamboo, with finger holes, leading
to a cow's-horn amplifier. A broomstraw was kept stuck in
this horn, to make some sort of refinement in the tone, and
from time to time Michaelis also poured *ouzo* into the top
finger-hole. He tried to explain the purpose of this to me

once, but my Greek wasn't half good enough, and anyway
he wanted to get back to playing.

I can't say what the mass of islanders thought about the
tourists. They must have been rather bewildered by us. If
they disliked us they were too polite to show it, and anyway
they all profited from our being there. I got a line on this
from two good informants. One was Vienoula Kousathanas,
who ran a weaving shop, well back in the town, with the
help of her daughters and several women of the neighborhood. In her teens she had been taken to Great Britain for a
few years by a godmother, so she spoke good English, and
she was a wise and talented woman into the bargain. She
herself had benefited a lot from the influx; she did fabrics
in subtle, sophisticated colors, and incoming tourists beat a
path to her — I suppose she was the best-known weaver in
all Greece. Her shop was a cheerful place, and the boys and
I used to hang around there, talking with her and her
daughters — especially with the eldest, Annouso, who was a
great beauty and an artist like her mother.

Vienoula did not personally like the changes that modern
times had brought to Mykonos, and she told us that she had
not gone to the waterfront in five years. "Sometimes I go
to a house near there, where my godfather lives," she said.
"But when I do I go by a back alley, which avoids the waterfront itself. Visitors ask me what restaurants there are good,
and I can't tell them. I cook myself, and I don't eat at
restaurants." But she added that nearly everyone in the
town was making extra money by renting rooms. "It used
to be that only the best houses here were rented," she said.
"But now the poorest rooms of the farmers are."

Later Annouso told us that everyone on Mykonos had
work now. "Everyone who wants it, that is," she added.

"We are very lucky. We are much better off than we used to be. And better off than the people on most other islands now."

My second informant was Costa Kampanis, the son of an old Mykoniat family, who had long worked on the mainland, as an official of the Bank of Greece, but who was now retired to his boyhood home. He was a convivial man, and at midday could usually be found in front of his pet café. He was, in fact, a prominent sight on the waterfront, and a picturesque one, with a red and handsome face crowned by a large Mykoniat tam o'shanter. Tourists were always guessing that he was a French painter, but he was a pure Mykoniat, descended on both sides from the family of Mado Mavroyeni, the local heroine of the Liberation War against the Turks — her statue graced the landward end of the waterfront's crescent, outside the Paralos Bar, which was the plush one for foreigners.

Kampanis's house lay a few yards inland, between this statue and the cafés. It had been built in 1739, and among other things it had part of an old mast for a ceiling-beam above the living-room. He told me this was a Mykoniat custom.

"In past centuries," he said, "the people of this island were great sailors. They sailed all through the Mediterranean and the Black Sea. Sometimes a mast would break, and if so they would usually replace it along the Russian coast, where they went to pick up grain and where timber was plentiful. Then they would sail back down through the Aegean, en route to another port. They might not be able to stop off at Mykonos itself, but the captain might still want to send his wife a greeting. So he would burn her name on a piece of the old mast and drop it overboard somewhere north of the island. With luck it would wash down on the northern coast, and whoever found it was duty bound to bring it to her. Later it would be put up in the house. The women lived a lonely life then, you see. They were also more important in the island's affairs than the men were, because the latter were away so much. The children, the houses, and the pieces of land were referred to by the wife's name, not the husband's."

In time Kampanis told me about many other things, too, including the island's economic ups and downs. Its best times, he said, had been in the period of Venetian dominance over the Cyclades (which ended in 1714). Its worst had been in the German occupation in the Second World War.

"People were not allowed to fish then," he explained, "because if a boat went out it might slip away to Asia. Trade between the islands was forbidden, too, so the people could not get things they needed, like olive oil. There was a bad famine. Many died on Mykonos, and the town was almost deserted. People went inland and lived on farms, if they could."

After the war things had been much better, he continued, but even so the Mykoniats had been poor until the tourist boom had started, a few years back.

"For myself," Kampanis said, "I don't like the changes since the war. Taxis have come, and motorcycles with side-cars, and I don't like to see them. But I must admit that everyone lives better now. In the old days if you saw a man with meat you knew it was Christmas or Easter. But now people have it every day. Children used to get only one piece of bread, some olive oil, and one fresh tomato. That would be their meal. But now they really eat, and they are much more lively. So why complain? I like to see the tourists come. They're good for us."

V

THE SEASON CONTINUES

In August I went on a purely native outing in Greece — a pilgrimage to the festival, or *paneghyri*, of the Virgin Mary on the island of Tinos. Tinos is one of the Cyclades, in the Aegean not far from Mykonos, and the shrine there is a great healing center — the Lourdes, it is often called, of the Orthodox world. Each year tens of thousands of Greeks, mainly poor ones, go there for the festival, which is on August fifteenth. I had heard of this huge gathering, unique in the Greek travel system, and Dicky and I — John Belmont had left by then — decided to go, though we understood we might have to sleep in the streets.

Wishing to make the trip somewhat in pilgrimage style, we packed two knapsacks, borrowed a couple of blankets from the Cecil Hotel in Kifissia, where we were staying again, and set out on foot for Raphina, the little port on Attica's east coast. Most of the boats for Tinos, as for other Aegean islands, leave from the Piraeus, but a couple of small, bush-league ones sail from Raphina in that direction — especially as August fifteenth draws near — on a more direct and midget course. This touches a few ports on the midway islands of Euboea and Andros, and it is nearly straight and only seventy miles long. The traffic on it is a miniature counterpart of that on the Aegean as a whole — just as the Aegean traffic, in turn, is a miniature of that on the Mediterranean.

We weren't sure what connections we could make, so we started three or four days before the festival was due. We got up early, taking advantage of the coolness, and spent five or six hours walking to Raphina itself — traveling through scenes that I knew from the spring and winter, but that were different now. The vineyards, especially — which had once been arrays of bare pruned stumps, and then of gushing tendrils — were now mature, with heavy clusters of pale grapes. We picked some along the way, and they were juicy and refreshing. We made Raphina at one o'clock. We had planned to rest, swim, and spend the night there, but we found a little passenger boat, the *Rena*, waiting at the jetty to set out in our direction. (She had once been Scandinavian, I judged later by the language on her instruments — a Danish inter-island boat, perhaps, or a Norwegian coaster — but now she was relegated to this secondary Aegean trade.) She planned to go as far as Batsi, a port on the south of Andros, where we were told we could spend the night and catch another ride, to Tinos itself, the next day. So we got a first-class cabin, then ate a lunch of sorts and took a nap, as the *Rena* headed out to sea.

Euboea, Andros, and Tinos are in a line — a partly sunken mountain range, I suppose — that runs southeast from the Greek mainland. We traveled down their southwest shores and thus were largely screened from the *meltemi*, but this shelter stopped for a while in the gap between Euboea and Andros. There we tossed a good deal, amid whitecaps — we felt the cool wind and saw rainbows in the spray. That gap is on the main route between Gi-

braltar and the Dardanelles; and much Turkish, and especially Russian, traffic goes through it. Now we saw a couple
of big hulks in the distance — a white one gleaming to our
northeast and a dark, shadowy one to our southwest, against
the lowering sun. But soon we had crossed the gap and were
in the lee of Andros. We ran along the hilly shore. The
Rena, being small, stayed close in, so we could see a good
deal on an intimate scale. It is always fun to sail along those
coasts — as it is fun to walk beside a shoreline — though
the Aegean islands repeat themselves a lot. Now, as we sat
on the deck, we were faced with steep brown hillsides, and
groves of silver olive trees, above the blue water — a sight
I had seen before that summer, and more than once.

We put in at one port, Gavrion, on Andros, and soon
after that came to another, Batsi, which was our terminus.
These ports, too, repeated themselves, and repeated a general Aegean theme, being built upward from curved water-
fronts and looking — with their tiers of bright little houses
— much like stage sets. We found a simple hotel at Batsi —
behind the little esplanade with its café tables — and stayed
there till the following afternoon. Like Gavrion — and like
Karystos, a Euboean port we had called at earlier — Batsi
was a fishing village heavily frequented, now in August, by
summer people out from Athens. They were all Greeks, so
far as I saw — not a foreigner in the lot — and they were
mostly mothers and children, plus a few husbands on vacation (it was a Friday then, still not the week-end). This
summer population seemed much the same as one would
find, say, in a sleepy, inexpensive Maine fishing village. All
morning we watched the children in their innocence —
swimming, learning how to row, admiring the fishermen,
asking about the catch, and starting on excursions. Then at
lunchtime we could imagine them hanging up their bathing

suits and tracking sand into the rented rooms — children of urban Athenians putting down roots in nature for a while, just as children of New Yorkers might. The life differed from the American model, though, in a few respects. There was a siesta in the early afternoon, when the crescent of beach by the town was bare and dead in its brightness. There was also more playing of cards — and backgammon — in public, at the cafés, than one would see in Maine. The Greeks adore these games, and when relaxing at their resorts will sit at them for hours.

At mid-afternoon that second day we boarded another little passenger boat, the *Moschanthe*, and at quarter to seven we made Tinos. As we pulled into the harbor we met a string of night-fishing dories going out on tow — five of them behind a launch, each with one fisherman amidships and two big lamps in the stern. They would stay out all night long, their lights twinkling in the darkness, and now they bounced freely and gaily as they went. Tinos was already crowded, though the *paneghyri* was scheduled only for the third day following. We couldn't find a room, but we happened on an old fisherman, named Yiannis Koulis, who said he had a beached caïque where we could sleep, at a total cost of one hundred drachmas, or a little over three dollars, till the festival was over. We took him up, invested twenty-five cents more in a clay water-jug, and installed ourselves. Caïques are the great native craft of the Aegean. They are broad, wooden, and buoyant; they come in all sizes and colors; and they mostly have engines now, along with their sails. This one was small, and it was beached at the edge of town, beside a breakwater. We spread our blankets on the two short bunks in its little fo'castle, and till the festival's end we lived there — we swam off the breakwater, we basked and dried our laundry on the deck, and we went often into town for meals and observations.

The crowd that finally showed up for the *paneghyri* was put at fifty thousand by some observers, and I suppose it was half that anyway. Everyone came on boats, of course. These converged from all directions, and I was told that normal shipping on the Aegean was disarranged for those few days. Early in the game I saw one little dark and rusty boat come in, listing extravagantly with leaning passengers; it discharged many of them, then backed out and hurried on with the remainder; and I learned it had come down from Salonika, in North Greece, en route to the Piraeus, and was making a fast detour for some pilgrim business. Other boats got completely off their routes, and one of them — the swift *Aigion* of the Typaldos Lines — was seen, when the great day dawned, to be running back and forth to the Piraeus like a ferry. Tinos has a lot of docking space by Aegean standards — rectangular, too, and up-to-date — and ships were constantly coming and going there, and whistling.

Of the passengers who got off, only a small minority were men. "There are mostly women here," a young Greek said to me one afternoon. "The husbands stay behind in Athens or the Piraeus, and have a good time." If men appeared, they were apt to be accompanying women — a son with a devout mother, for example. Some women were fulfilling vows. Some came off their boats on hands and knees, and continued that way for hundreds of yards, up a stone or concrete street, till they reached the church of the Virgin itself. I saw one woman proceeding thus with a small boy astride her, like a jockey. I saw invalids — a hunchback girl on the arm of another woman, for instance, and a blind man on the arm of someone else. Many had plainly come in hopes of a

cure, but the vast majority were there, it seemed, for just
the vague holiness of the occasion, and the getting together.
Mass *paneghyria* have taken place for thousands of years in
Greece and Asia Minor, and this one at Tinos is the greatest
of them all today. It has special significance for the Aegean
— it is the great Aegean fair, so to speak, much as the
festivals at Delos must have been in classical times. To me it
was also like an old-time Fourth of July in the States — a
really old-time one, when we too were poor. I saw grand-
mothers washing naked babies at the waterside; and the
breakwater by our caïque was crowded, in the noontimes,
like Coney Island — especially as the *meltemi* failed then,
for a day or two, and the scene grew hot.

The bulk of the pilgrims had no roofs to sleep under, and
they gathered mainly in the compound around the church.
It was paved in pebble mosaic, on which they spread rugs
and blankets. Soon these touched each other, edge to edge,
so the place was covered entirely; and at night the sleeping
bodies fitted beside each other like puzzle pieces. By day
the same bodies sat and ate on the same patches. I saw a
woman preparing a mess of sea-urchins on her blanket, and
I saw another with a live chicken tethered there. Still others
had jugs of wine and baskets of fruit or vegetables. Many
were fasting, to some extent, till the big day itself, for which
they were keeping these provisions ready. Meanwhile hawkers circulated among them, selling nougat, turkish delight,
pistachio nuts, and rolls.

The provisioning of the island for those few days, a huge
job, was done efficiently, but also exploitatively and rather
inartistically — without much grace or flavor — by certain
of the Tinians, a race whom many other Greeks denounce
as pilgrim-bleeders. I didn't study the logistics much, but I
kept running into them. The restaurants grew terribly

crowded as time passed; then certain kinds of food ran out, though others lasted. Just about all the restaurants seemed to have squids for sale till near the very end, though they are smallish creatures that must be gathered separately from different places. Veal and lamb, on the other hand, seemed to run out early.* Watermelons were in good supply, for caïques loaded with them came and tied up at the quays. Flour was well stocked, too, but the baking of it seemed to be a strain — on the next-to-last day I stopped in at a bakery, and three or four men were kneading dough groggily there, as if about to drop.

Much was sold besides food, of course, even profane things like cloth and shoes — which helped us to see how shrines, in classical days, had so often given birth to markets. As for sacred objects, there was a good traffic in beads, candles, cheap icons, and the silver replicas of body members that are used as votive offerings. Many of the candles, also for offerings, were taller than a man. These things were sold in stalls, for the most part, along the main street climbing to the church. That stretch was lined by hawkers and beggars, many of them invalids — crippled sellers of candles, for instance, and blind musicians.

The *meltemi* rose again, strongly, on the night before the festival. It tore at our caïque — tore at everything — and chilled the air. It also livened things, and that morning there were wild waves, whitecaps, and brightness in the harbor. The flags on land and on the ships were flapping brilliantly — and ships kept coming in, in the early morning, to tie up at the jetty and await the homeward flood of pilgrims. They whistled and their flags flew, and by the end ten or a dozen of them were lying there — the *Aigion*, the *Marilena*, the

---

* Veal and lamb are taboo in Orthodox fasting, whereas many seafoods are not. This alone may account for the apparent imbalance.

Elli Toyia, the *Rena*, the *Stella*, the *Moschanthe*, the *Glaros*,
the *Aikaterini*, the *Myrtidiotissa*, others — the dainty, sometimes rusty, queens of the Aegean.

Meanwhile the crowd surged on the esplanade and up and
down the streets. They surged till halfway through the
morning; then police began to hold them still and rope off
places. A square was roped off on the esplanade itself, and
officials began to gather there, together with a navy band
and a boy-scout one. I found a place on one of the ships —
on its upper deck — overlooking this square, but I saw only
the esplanade itself; I could not look far up the two streets
toward the church, though these had been roped off, too,
for a procession. I stood and watched the crowd. The Greek
Prime Minister, Constantinos Caramanlis, was scheduled to
come, and soon he did come — riding through the harbor
on a launch — and the whistles blew. He landed. Then the
procession itself came on — a supposedly miraculous icon,
in a litter, accompanied by vested priests. Higher up the hill
— I later learned from Dicky, who was there — the icon
had been carried over a line of sick people, who were lying
in the street. It was a moving sight, he said, but I missed it.
I only saw the icon with its priests come down to the clear-
ing. Then there were services and chanting, and some band
music and a little speaking. Then the ceremony was over.
The Prime Minister sailed off, amid flags and whistles. The
crowd began to melt, and the ships to load and pull away.
And we were with them.

After that excursion I based at the Cecil for a further
spell, while Dicky did some traveling on his own. Kifissia,
as a hill resort, was going full blast then. In the winter I had
seen it nearly deserted, then in the spring it had begun to fill,
and now its season was at the peak. The Cecil was jammed
with Greeks from Athens, and even a few from Egypt (in

former years there had been many such, but now, with the
Nasser regime, the Egyptian Greeks are poorer; many have
left, and those who remain have trouble getting their money
out). The Kifissia nights were sweet and cool, unlike the
nights of Athens; and the place was a fairyland in the evenings, with its bright-lit taverns and cafés. It had rustling
aspens and babbling irrigation channels, which ran uncovered next the streets. I used to walk by these, and their sound
gave a feel of Central Asia, where the towns too have aspens,
and poplars, and ditches running open — I used to think,
perhaps incorrectly, that this effect was a sign of Turkish
influence on Greece. Another Kifissia treat I used to think
rather Turkish was the prevalence there of horse-drawn
carriages, waiting by the parks to take the guests on calls or
joyrides. Those carriages and their drivers were a dying
race, I fear. They had only two good summer months of
business to balance against a long, thin winter, and they were
up against taxis, buses, and all that. Yet still they were hanging on, and waiting in long lines beneath the trees. I loved
the smell of the horses as I passed, and I liked to talk with
the drivers, haltingly, in my bad Greek and their bad
English.

Some of the Kifissia *tavernas* were excellent, and I went
especially to a new one, which had opened the winter before
and was very popular. It had a cool garden with gravel in it,
and whitewashed tree-trunks, and canaries singing high in
cages. I used to go early in the evening and order simple
dishes — *pilaphi*, for instance, the garnished rice that is another hint of Central Asia — of the *polao* or *pilaff* that is
served all through that region.

Sometimes — not often — I would tour the cafés that
were near the Cecil; I would sample the *ouzos* there, and
compare their prices, their sizes, and their accompanying
hors d'oeuvres, which varied markedly from place to place.

But usually I would have dinner in the Cecil and go to bed. I would dine about eight-thirty, which is very early for Greece. My only companions then, on the dining-terrace behind the hotel, were apt to be little children and their governesses — or perhaps a couple of old ladies would be taking a *peripato*, or stroll, there, on the theory, I suppose, that meal-time hadn't begun at all. Some of the governesses were British, teaching the Queen's tongue to little Greeks, along with their conception of table manners. I have met several of these British girls around in Greece; they are pretty and adventurous, as a rule — not at all like old-style nannies — and they must be paid well.

The adult Greeks at the Cecil, in the summer throng, were well dressed, inactive, and often pretty elderly. They played cards, drank little cups of coffee, and talked. They dined late and enjoyed the coolness.

I went to Athens often, usually on the train, which was clean and pleasant. I saw friends there and did errands and a little sight-seeing. The Acropolis is not much fun to visit in the daytime in the summer — it is hot and glary then — but under a full moon it is wonderful. The tones of the marble are perfect in the moonlight, and so are the sharp lines of the architecture. On the four nights closest to the moon's fullness the Acropolis is open till midnight, and hordes of people go there then. They wander slowly by the Parthenon and Erechtheion, thinking their thoughts. The women in the crowd are apt to take their shoes off, I have noticed, and wander silently. The stone of the Acropolis itself has strange old corrugations and cuttings in it, but its surface is smooth and shiny, and in the moon it gleams. The visitors steal about there, avoiding one another, till twelve o'clock approaches, when the guards sound bells and whistles to get them out.

On other nights the Acropolis is used for a *Son et Lumière* performance, of the kind that is common now in western Europe — especially, I understand, among the châteaux of the Loire. Changing searchlights, in warm pastel colors, are played on the old temples, while paying customers watch from a nearby hill, the Pnyx, and listen to a sound track — in Greek, French, or English — with musical accompaniment. The sound track is corny in the extreme, but the lights have the merit of showing off the great old architecture in unexpected ways. Of course non-paying tourists may enjoy it, too, from different parts of the city. Thanks to searchlights, the Acropolis points Athens up by night now, as well as day.

In August a so-called Festival of Athens was in progress, too. It was held in the Odeon of Herodes Atticus, a Roman-period theater that stands beside the Acropolis; and it offered a series of orchestral music, old Greek plays, and some more modern plays with a Greek background, like the *Phédre* of Racine. I saw the *Iphigeneia in Tauris* of Euripides there. It was splendidly staged — like the other old Greek plays I had seen earlier at Epidaurus — but this theater, being in the Roman style, seemed less appropriate than the one at Epidaurus. Instead of moving in a big full circle of space, as at Epidaurus, the chorus was cramped into a smaller semi-circle, facing a stage of hard, imposing stone on a level with their heads. They danced and chanted nicely, but they seemed less blended with the main action than in the proper Greek theater. The influence of modern Athens kept intruding on this performance, too, whereas those at Epidaurus had been lost in nature. The stage was backed by a very high, crumbly old buff wall, with a rhythmic Italian pattern of windows, doors, arches, and niches in it; this gave some protection, yet traffic noise came through it nonetheless.

Of course the theater was right in Athens — more convenient than Epidaurus — and that was a boon. It was also a boon — for me at least — to have life and action put into the old structure. That summer too, in September, I saw some inter-Balkan games in the Athenian stadium. This is *the* old stadium — long and narrow — of the classical city. It was enlarged in Roman times — but not changed in form — by the same Herodes Atticus who built the Odeon. Then it was recently fixed up again, in 1896, so that the first modern Olympic games could be held in it. It is normally a rather fierce eyeful of white marble, but when I went to these Balkan games — it was early evening — the place was full of flags, color, athletes, and a cheering crowd. I didn't really follow who was winning — Greek, Yugoslav, Turk, etc. — but I loved the warmth and heartbeat of it.

Late in August I flew for a week-end to the island of Rhodes, together with some Greek and American friends who had a plane at their disposal. The course to Rhodes slants down southeastward, across the Aegean — the trip is short, and we flew it low. I had a fine chance to look down on islands that I had previously been studying at sea-level — on Mykonos, Delos, Tinos, Naxos, Amorgos, Patmos, Kos, Kalymnos, and others. They seemed rather stark and wrinkled from the air, and definitely more eroded — more peneplaned, in the technical word — than do the dry-land mountains of which they are a continuation. I can't give a reason for this, unless they have been deprived much longer of their forest cover — or perhaps have a different history of sea erosion. They did look bare, anyway, and they were a sort of reddish brown — a red-fox color — as they lay there in the dark blue sea.

On Rhodes our party stayed at a resort called the Mira Mare, which was interesting and where we had a good time

together, though it was not a spot I would have chosen on
my own. It was purely a beach resort, a place to rest and
get away from it all. It occupied a strip of shoreline — self-
contained, and cut off from the rest of Rhodes by a high
fence, thus making it a compound where one could stay for
days, or even weeks, without venturing out. The resort had
been first established by the Italians, I think, when they controlled Rhodes before the Second World War, but had recently been much expanded, and this process was still going
on — a chambermaid told me that the Mira Mare had had
fewer than a hundred beds the year before, but now had
two hundred and fifty.

The beds were in *cabañas*, for the most part, one of which
I had all to myself. It had a bathroom and a smallish terrace,
besides its spacious bedroom. It lay back from the beach,
behind a row of other *cabañas*, and it was connected with
these, and with *cabañas* to the right and left, where my
friends were staying, by open paths. The beach itself was
gravelly — poor, in that respect, by Greek standards — but
it was a pleasant place to nap and dip, and nap again. The
compound had a big restaurant, dance-floor, bar, shops, and
so on, along with a couple of subsidiary cafés, a swimming-
pool, and a public-address system. It was heavily patronized
by German tourists of the richer sort, but also had a sprinkling of other nationalities. It has been used by movie actors,
too — staying there when making films on Rhodes.*

(There are several other such beach resorts in Greece,
though I paid little attention to them in my travels, as they
were cut off from the Greek life I was interested in. There

---

* Two American films, *Surprise Package* and *The Guns of Navarone*,
were made on Rhodes in 1959 and 1960, and their companies stayed at
the Mira Mare *en bloc*. These included Anthony Quinn, Gregory Peck,
Yul Brynner, and others.

is another posh one, called Astiria, on the coast near Athens
— a bit too near the Athens airport — where one may go
to swim or may rent a *cabaña* to live in if forehanded; the
waiting-list is long there. This and the Mira Mare are for the
fairly rich, but there are many others for the less so, these
being patronized especially by young people, secretaries and
so on, from all over northwest Europe — they come and
have a cheap, restful, sunny vacation in them before returning to their foggy homelands. I dropped in on one such
place, Kyllini, during the summer. It was way over on the
west side of the Peloponnesus, looking off toward Italy, and
could be reached by rail or by a long road through some
moors — it was very isolated. I was shown a little bungalow
there, for two people, with a toilet and shower, that cost
only four dollars a day, per person, with full board. There
were also cheaper bungalows and tents, plus a common
open-air restaurant and café, plus things like bamboo
benches, here and there, under pines. The manager said that
the place's capacity is three hundred and fifty, and that it
does a good business with Greeks, other Europeans, and
some Canadians and Americans. These last, though, I think,
are likely to be people stationed in Athens, not long-range
tourists. The long-range ones, as a rule, come to sample all
of Greece's attractions, not just the sun and sea, however
lovely.)

On the Sunday morning of that week-end I left the Mira
Mare and took a long walk through the nearby countryside.
Rhodes seemed quite different from the other islands that I
knew. It had a good deal of vegetation, for one thing,
though this was dry and almost smoldering now — it was
tawny in the sun. The landscape seemed more developed —
as to roads, water mains, etc. — than some other Greek ones

I knew, and I wondered if this might reflect Italian influence; the Fascists made a show-place out of Rhodes, I have
gathered. The vegetation seemed relatively southern-looking
— it had date-palms in it, which I had never seen in Attica
or the Cyclades.* I imagined, too, that the people looked
more dark and supine — more Eastern — than the mainland
Greeks, but this may have been a subjective feeling on my
part, for I was mindful that Rhodes had been especially open
to Middle Eastern, and even African, contacts through the
ages.

At noon I stopped and had a watermelon in a café run by
a Turk — the first Turk I had ever spoken with in Greece.
Turks were evacuated from most of the country in the early
'twenties, after a catastrophic Greco-Turkish war, but not
from Rhodes, because the Italians held it then; and there are
still some left there, though they are dwindling. This man's
manner and language — in talking with another Turk —
seemed harsher, somehow, than that of the Greeks to whom
I was accustomed. But again my feeling may have been
subjective. I walked all that morning, anyway, indulging
my fancies, then went back to the Mira Mare and to hibernation on the beach. And on Monday morning we flew back
to Athens.

On September first I moved into the city; Dicky returned
from his travels then; and another son, Chris, aged twenty-
three, came to join us briefly from Iran, where he was studying. I had taken a little flat in Athens for the rest of the year,
and it was a pleasant place; but it was crowded by the three
of us and also hot in that weather, so I rented a Volkswagen
and we took short excursions in the daytime. We went

* I am told that dates grow on the island of Aegina, near Athens.

usually to the beaches of Attica — either to the southern
ones, near Athens, which were crowded, or to the eastern
ones, looking off toward Asia, which were not.

We swam, loafed, ate at *tavernas*, and saw the country.
We also visited some ruins, notably those at Eleusis and
Sounion, which were within an hour's drive. Eleusis is linked
with the wheat Goddess Demeter, whose daughter Perseph-
one was kidnapped by Hades, but was later allowed to make
seasonal returns from the underworld — the legend has
overtones of vegetable immortality, of life rising again and
again from the earth. Eleusis was the scene of the Eleusinian
mysteries, into which the adult men of Greece, and later of
Rome, were initiated. Alas for us today, the mysteries were
well kept; even the copious travel-writer Pausanias — an
initiate — refrained from writing about the sanctuary's
buildings, which are said to have been screened from public
view by a high wall. It is generally thought that initiates
were assured of immortality, in some dramatic way, by
representations of the Demeter myth — the experience
seems to have had a great effect on many of them, and to
have been a factor in the morale of ancient times. One cannot get much appreciation of this by visiting the ruins now,
but at least the site is a pleasant one, near the seaside —
ancient even as classical sites go — and with a nice little
museum on a height there.

During Byzantine times, Christians made a great effort to
deface the shrine and rob it of prestige. This was a common
occurrence in Greece — pagan shrines were often vandal-
ized by Christians, or attempts were made to rechannel the
forces there by building a church on the site. But at Eleusis
the work went especially far. Whole massive structures were
pulled down flat, and Byzantine crosses were carved on
many individual stones.

Sounion is southeast of Athens, on the very point of Attica — the cape that looks out at the Cyclades. There are two old sanctuaries — of Athena and Poseidon — there, the latter being the most visited now because of its situation. It stands right on the headland, which is high — the simple ruins of a fine chaste Doric temple, looking out magnificently above the water. It is best seen in a fair amount of solitude, but the time we went there — late one afternoon — it was crowded with tourists, three or four busloads of them. There happened, that day, to be a weird, spectacular cherry-red sunset over the island of Aegina — twenty-five miles to Sounion's west — and the tourists were lining up with cameras, like a firing-squad, to shoot it. At least they seemed to be enjoying the place, in every way — gazing out to sea and studying, and fondling, the old marble of the temple. People pat old temple marble. They run their hands along it and then slap it. It is sculpture, and it cries out to be touched.

In that period the three of us went also for a week-end to the island of Hydra, just off the Peloponnesian east coast. Next to Mykonos it is the most popular with foreign tourists of all the smaller Greek islands. Hydra invites comparison with Mykonos, too, and I — a Mykonos fan — saw it mainly in that way. Hydra has the advantage of being handier to Athens — three hours' boat travel as against, say, seven for Mykonos — and this can be important. Its seaport also has a remarkable appeal for the eye. It is the quintessence of all the better Aegean ports — a high, spectacular amphitheater of town spreading upward from a rounded harbor — like a mosaic of houses on a screen around the viewer. Some of the houses are exceptionally big and elegant, too. They were built by Hydriot ship-owners who made huge fortunes, before 1815, by running the blockade imposed by Britain on Napoleon — they would take supplies from elsewhere in the Mediterranean, or the Black Sea, and run them to Spain, or the south of France, at a big profit. Later they sacrificed nearly all these gains on behalf of the Greek War of Independence — in which Hydriot shipping played a crucial role — but meanwhile they had built the houses, and these remain. They are spacious and well proportioned, with big rooms and terraces. They have wooden ceilings, with molding-patterns in relief, and some still have fine furniture and fittings. Others have been given up as homes, because of modern economics — one is now a government hostel for artists — but whether homes or not, they still remain there and adorn the town, which must be one of the handsomest on earth.

Aside from these points, I think Mykonos is a more enjoyable place. Hydra has no decent beaches, for one thing, and this is a real drawback, though swimming off the rocks can be fun, of course. Nor has it a gentle countryside for walking, like that of Mykonos. It is steep, rocky, and forbidding — one must either walk along its shoreline, on a rigid course, or clamber up the heights, and both these ways can pall. More important still is the temper of the people — on Mykonos they are cordial, but on Hydra they are gruff, though they will consent to say hello.

A Greek lady on Hydra once tried to explain their attitude to me. "You see, they are Albanians here," she said. "Many Albanians came down to Greece in the past few centuries, and they settled Hydra and some other regions, like the rural parts of Attica, that were thinly populated then. Albanians are famous for being aloof with foreigners. Their attitude is just opposite to the Greek one, which is what you find on Mykonos."

"What villages in Attica are especially Albanian?" I
asked.

"Most of them. There are some exceptions, but nearly all
are that."

"But I've walked through many of them, and they're
friendly."

"Ah, yes, but they've been under lots of Athenian influence, you see, and the people have learned Greek manners.
The people on Hydra have been isolated, and they've
stayed the same."

Be all that as it may, local attitudes needn't matter much,
really, to casual visitors, and anyway it is certainly better to
see Hydra as Hydra, not — in my fashion — as a negative
of Mykonos. Many painters and writers live happily there.
Hadjikyriakos Ghika, the best-known painter in Greece, is
an Hydriot native and works there busily, as do others.
Chris, Dicky, and I had two delightful evenings in the cafés
there, too, consorting with all kinds of people — aside from
Greek artists and intellectuals, I remember especially three
foreign writers: an Australian, a Swede, and an American
Negro. The Australian, George Johnston, has lived on
Hydra for several years now, and he and his wife have both
written prolifically there — she has written a book about
Hydra itself called *Peel Me a Lotus*, which seems a good
tag-line for this whole foreign occupation of the islands.

VI

THE BIG SEA TOUR

I first saw Lena Politis in circumstances that suggested — I thought — an old Greek slave-market. With Chris, Dicky, and scores of other tourists I was standing in a saloon of the S.S. *Aigion* (née the *Princess Alice* in Glasgow around 1900). It was a Monday evening in September; we had just embarked on an Aegean cruise that would last till Saturday morning; and the "cruise-manager" was giving an introductory talk to the English-speaking tourists — the French- and German-speakers would come later. The manager was a small thin man, with hollow cheeks, who might have come from a George Price cartoon — when he went ashore, later on, he always wore a big white solar topee, an item of dress that has otherwise almost disappeared from European heads. He gave his talk, then said he would introduce our guide, and Lena stepped forward. She had brown hair and blue eyes. She bowed, and we looked at her (I thought) as buyers might have looked at some new offering in the Delos market around 100 B.C. She didn't say much then — she just smiled wistfully — and I wasn't greatly impressed by her. Nor did the session last long. Class was dismissed, and we pupils hurried up to the bar for an *ouzo* before dinner.

The next morning, when we stepped ashore at the Cretan port of Herakleion, Lena was wearing a blue straw hat, a red-and-white striped cotton jersey, a blue summer skirt, and a pair of blue espadrilles. It was a simple outfit, but workmanlike and attractive. We passengers — one or two hundred of us — left the jetty together in a fleet of buses, these taking us a few miles into the countryside and then dumping us, in a big open space, outside the old Minoan Palace of Cnossos. At that stage the guides sorted us out, standing apart like shepherds and calling to us. "English-speaking group this way," Lena called out, "English-speaking group this way." And she waved a piece of paper to catch our eyes.

The French-speaking guide, standing in another spot, was old and rather distinguished-looking, though I came to find her pedantic as I eavesdropped on her, in snatches, during the next few days. The German-speaking guide was young, apple-cheeked, and forceful. Lena was calm. She got us around her like ducklings, then led us to a shady place and briefed us on the Minoan civilization—on how it had flourished in the second millennium B.C., how it had borrowed a good deal from Egypt, how the mainland Greeks had probably come to dominate it, and how it had ended suddenly and mysteriously around 1400 — because of foreign invasion, she was inclined to think, though she did not press this view on us. She was detached and un-dogmatic, and it was clear from the outset that she knew her stuff. Perhaps she exaggerated the evidence for Greek dominance in Crete, but then all Greek guides seem chau-vinistic about their past. Otherwise she gave a straight story, and a well-organized one. She spoke quietly and with hu-mor, and she had a secret smile.

Later she took us to the Palace of King Minos itself. It

is a big rambling place, much restored by the late Sir Arthur Evans, the rich and brilliant Englishman who excavated it — who discovered the Minoan civilization, really, for the modern world. Evans caused walls to be rebuilt, colors to be reapplied, and murals to be repainted, all in an effort to recapture the old Palace's appearance — he used cement beams, painted yellow with a grain pattern, to represent the ancient, vanished wooden ones. Restoration is a controversial thing in Greece — even when expertly done — and I have heard archaeologists call Cnossos a Disneyland. I didn't mind it, though — I like my ruins comprehensible — and Lena didn't seem to either.

"There has been criticism of Sir Arthur's work," she said. "Some like it and some don't. But at least it was done carefully. The reconstruction of the murals was a hard job, especially. They were built up from tiny fragments, on the basis of Sir Arthur's knowledge, by a gifted young artist who worked with him. The artist also went by the look of the murals when they were first excavated. The material was crumbly, and much of it turned to dust when the air got at it, so he studied it fast, in that brief moment, and reproduced what he saw."

We began walking through the Palace, as restored. It had red walls, often, and many pillars, these being red, black, or white in color, and tapering outward as they rose.

"We don't know why they were this shape," Lena said. "Perhaps the form came from trees, originally, placed upside down so the roots wouldn't sprout. Or perhaps the builders made them narrow at the bottom so there would be more space there, at the human level, for people to move around."

The murals had the same colors, predominantly — red, black, and white — as the pillars, along with a good deal of

blue. What we saw now, on the Palace walls, were copies
pure and simple — the reconstructed originals being in
the museum at Herakleion. The paintings showed Cretan
youths and women, the former being red of skin — like
the traditional idea of American Indians — and narrow-
waisted, perhaps because of girdles that they wore. The
women were also thin-waisted, paler than these men, and
elegantly dressed and coifed, but with their breasts entirely
bare. "The *décolletage* was very daring," Lena said dis-
creetly — she turned out to be a master of such understatement.

Pictures of bulls — a motif that seems to permeate Cnossos — recurred in the murals. One showed a scene of the
"bull-dance," which has puzzled and fascinated the experts
since it was found. In the mural a young male athlete was
somersaulting through the horns of a bull — which was
charging straight at him — and then bouncing off its back
into the arms of a girl assistant. Certain toreadors and
American bulldoggers, Lena said, have called this stunt almost impossible, yet scholars believe that it was regularly
practised at Cnossos. Many think that Spanish bull-fighting
is descended from it. Some think, too, that the legend of
Theseus slaying the Minotaur arose from it, and this later
theory has been woven into the novel *The King Must Die*,
where readers may find a speculative explanation of the
whole thing.

We kept on going through the Palace, with the *Aigion*'s
French-speaking group a little behind us. The place had
many chambers, on different levels, plus big underground
storerooms. It had a grand stairway — still intact without
much restoration — that went around and around a light-
well and must have been an engineering triumph for its
time. The Palace was ingeniously planned, too, with a view

to coolness in certain important rooms, these being built
low down in the structure — far from the sunny roofs —
but with good light and ventilation contrived for them.
There was also a throne-room — with a reconstruction of
the first throne of Europe, Lena said — and a royal bathroom containing, apparently, a flush toilet.

Lena dwelt on these marvels a good deal — partly, I
think, out of pride in the Minoans, who were so nearly
Greek, and partly, perhaps, because Greek guides are
taught, in their training, to stress engineering wonders and
big achievements when talking to Americans. No guide has
ever confessed this to me, but I have been told by other
Greeks that it is so. With French tourists — according to
these informants — guides are supposed to dwell on aesthetic or spiritual things, with Germans they are supposed
to give minutely detailed facts, and with Americans they
are supposed to bring out the bigger-and-better aspects of
antiquity. I don't think Lena was at all mechanical in applying such rules, though. She had a feeling for the old civilization. One of our group commented on the small scale of
the Palace rooms — they *were* small, by modern standards
of monumentality — and Lena questioned why they should
have been especially grand or luxurious. She did this tactfully, though; she was always tactful. There was a bump-
tious old Englishman in our group who liked to air his
views on things, and Lena complimented him on his knowledge and drew him out. She was like a hostess.

After doing the Palace we stopped in a nearby tourist
pavilion to have soft drinks and rest awhile, then we got
into buses again and returned to Herakleion, to the museum
there. Once inside it we faced a bad traffic situation as there
was another cruise boat, with three or four language groups,

on hand besides our own. Each guide had to keep her flock
apart from the others — which involved a good deal of
waiting — and even so the halls resounded, somewhat, with
conflicting commentaries. They were not too loud, though,
and the museum itself is one of the best in Greece — in the
whole Mediterranean, for that matter — with a fine collection intelligently, though simply, displayed, and showing
the extant works of the Minoan civilization.

That civilization was maritime, rich, and cosmopolitan,
and it had links with older ones to the south and east, especially that of Egypt. It also had periods when luxury —
even decadence — prevailed, so that jewelry, cosmetics, and
other aspects of high fashion were much developed. Case
after case in the museum was full of the results, and Lena
discoursed on them with relish, as she did on the elegant,
gossipy women's court manners shown in the murals — this
appreciation of the very urbane is one more reason, I think,
why women make better guides than men in Greece.

Of course the museum was by no means a strictly fem-
inine affair. It had superb metal-work, in cups and bowls;
superb pottery; and superb painting especially. This last —
much of it on the pottery — was light, sketchy, impression-
istic, and full of nature. It seems true that the Minoan arts
were closely tied up with Egypt, but this painting lacked
the ponderous quality that one associates with most Egyptian work — except for the light, gay things that were done
under the heretic King Ikhnaton. Lightness and gaiety were
the keynote, one might say, of Minoan painting, with its
ducks and doves and porpoises — and octopuses and flowers.
The Minoan culture, as preserved in that museum, was an
exquisite bloom, and it was the beginning, so far as we can
tell, of sophisticated art in Europe.

We all went back to the *Aigion* for lunch, then in the afternoon many of us went by bus to Phaestos, another Minoan site near Crete's south coast. In general this was much like Cnossos — except that it hadn't been restored — and the trip down was like other late-summer trips in Greece — through tawny valleys, albeit lovely ones. The trip was long, too, and we didn't get back to the boat till late afternoon. We went aboard at once, the boat cast off, and we set out for Rhodes — our next day's landfall — the minute we were all accounted for.

A numbered "landing-card" — a sort of tag — had been assigned to each of us at the voyage's start. On going ashore we were supposed to take the tags with us, and on coming back we were supposed to hang them up on numbered hooks on a board. The cards symbolized us — they almost *were* us. Where we went they went, and by looking at the gaps on the board the cruise-manager could tell, theoretically, just which of us were still astray. We were highly organized — we had to be, I suppose, for our survival as a group — and each of us had a sixteen-page booklet with minute instructions on our stops and other activities — even instructions on the instructions: e.g. "Will you please read *tomorrow's program tonight*, before going to bed! as we disembark early tomorrow morning."

The boys and I shared a four-bed cabin, and we sat together in the dining-room with a young Dane, two middle-aged Italian ladies, and a Jewish brother and sister who lived, respectively, in England and Israel, and who had joined in Greece for a holiday. They had been born in Germany, but their family had left there before Hitler came to power. Now the sister, a widow, was an Israeli social worker, and the brother was a London accountant. He was also a keen student of the Bible — New and Old Testaments alike —

and a delightful man to talk with. The sister was interesting, too, as was the young Dane. The latter had been an official, for a couple of years, in Greenland, and he had much to say about that strange outpost of Norse empire with its Eskimos and deep ice. The Italian ladies were pleasant, but I had a language problem with them, and they also seemed un-alert — placid and bourgeois — by temperament.

The cruise had drawn a mixed lot of people. Early in the game we fell in with a couple of delightful Englishmen — one was an estate manager and the other a teacher at London University — who had read a great deal about the Mediterranean, who had lived in other parts of it, and who were keen, in a well-informed way, about everything we saw. There was also a young, very blonde Dutch girl, with a pigtail and amber eyes; a forceful, interesting White Russian woman from New York; a Siamese diplomat's wife and her mother; a French bride with a lovely figure who hovered, in a bikini, near the ship's tiny swimming-pool; and a Hollywood-type American who wore a cigar and several cameras and who was accompanied by a painted, rather pretty, languid blonde, several inches taller than himself, in flowered slacks — she looked like a chorus girl, and she seldom left the boat for anything but shopping. These were among the more conspicuous passengers, and there were also many inert, less interesting ones to make a background for them.

There were not, alas, many young people on the *Aigion*, though the boys learned that there was an oversupply of young French girls, ironically, on the *Kriti*, a sister-ship that sailed along on our same schedule. Three ships were on this schedule, in fact — the *Aigion* and the *Kriti*, of the Typaldos Lines, and the *Semiramis*, which was operated, though not owned, by the Greek government tourist office. The *Kriti* carried the overflow of the *Aigion* and was subsidiary to it, though it kept apart and had its own guides, including an Italian-speaking one. It seemed natural for these two ships to be going around the islands neck and neck, but it was puzzling that the *Semiramis* should be with them. Even one cruise ship, if well filled, can swamp the shore facilities of a small island, yet week after week that summer the *Aigion* and *Semiramis* — with or without the *Kriti* — made the circuit more or less together.

The circuit consisted of Crete on Tuesday, after a full night's sail from the Piraeus; then Rhodes on Wednesday, after another full night's sail; then Kos and Patmos on Thursday, each after a short run; then Delos and Mykonos on Friday, followed by a night trip back to the start. In between Rhodes and Kos the *Aigion* added Halicarnassus, or Budrum, a small port on the Turkish mainland, though perhaps she did this largely to show that she was faster than the *Semiramis*.

There seemed to be a good deal of rivalry between the two. "The *Semiramis* is smaller than the *Aigion*," Lena once remarked to a few of us. "They say, too, that the food is not so good." She shrugged noncommittally. "But I don't really know," she added.

Actually I had traveled on the *Semiramis* too — I had taken a cruise on her in 1959, with still a third son, Peter. I had found her a more enjoyable boat than the *Aigion*, but had found her guiding service inferior to Lena's. As to food, I don't think either had much to boast of except at lunchtime, when they both served fair hors d'oeuvres — dinner on each was the usual imitation West European fare. Both stayed late at Rhodes and Mykonos, however, so one might dine there, and the faster *Aigion* stayed late at Patmos, too. The prices of the two boats were competitive — from roughly fifty dollars a passage up to something a good deal higher, if one had a de luxe cabin.

We made Rhodes at breakfast-time on Wednesday — the town of Rhodes, that is, on the north end of the island of that name — and we tied up in the little harbor there. The town's core is a medieval settlement, built by the Crusaders, which has walls and battlements of porous buff stone. A big wall with a couple of gates stands right over the quays, in fact, and soon we were walking toward this in the wake of Lena, who that morning wore a lilac dress, with a lilac scarf on her head. She got us into the town — and into the shade — and briefed us on the island's complex history. She quoted Pindar on how Rhodes had been born of the love between Helios, the Sun God, and the nymph Rhoda. Then she went into the story of Greek domination over the island, from Mycenean times down to Alexander the Great, after which it had became a battleground of influence between Alexander's Macedonian and Egyptian — Ptolemaic — successors. It was in this Hellenistic period that the Colossus had been built.

"In 303 B.C. Demetrios the Besieger, a Macedonian, tried to take the city," Lena said. "He used all kinds of siege machinery against the walls, but the people held out. Finally he gave up and went away, and out of respect for the city's courage he left the siege machines behind him, as a present. The Rhodians sold them, and with the proceeds they built the Colossus. It was a hundred and five feet tall and was a statue of Helios, with metal rays coming out of its head. Later it was destroyed by an earthquake, and the Oracle of Delphi said it should not be rebuilt. So it lay here till the sixth century A.D., when the Arabs took it away."

The Arabs and the Byzantine Empire had had a long struggle over Rhodes, which had been interrupted by the Crusaders' arrival. The Knights of Saint John, coming in 1300, had dug in especially well — they had kept hostels on the island for pilgrims and others en route to the Holy Land. This regime had lasted till the conquest of Rhodes, in 1521, by Suleiman the Magnificent, after which it had been Turkish until 1912, when the Italians had got it, yielding it finally to Greece in 1948.

Part of the Crusader establishment has been turned into a museum — mainly for classical sculpture — and Lena took us through this now. Then she led us on to another medieval structure, the old Palace of the Grand Master — of the Knights of Saint John — which the Italians had restored, and fixed up considerably, during their occupation — it had been the headquarters of Cesare di Vecchi, the Fascist governor of the Dodecanese. We found the palace spacious — with many large halls — but half a dozen other flocks of tourists were also there, which involved us in some backing and filling, with guides calling out to one another, in Greek, so as to co-ordinate our movements.

The floors of several rooms had mosaics on them, and we were instructed not to step on these, but to pass around on the narrow spaces framing them. They were old work, Lena said, done just before or just after the time of Christ, and they had been collected by the Italians in the Dodecanese, especially Kos.

"It is a great pity," she added. "The mosaics were transported here by experts and installed at much expense. Yet if the Italians were still here they would be wearing them out in a few decades, because they used these halls as reception rooms, with people walking through them all the time. Of course the mosaics were made to be walked on, but not by hard modern shoes. We would like to put them back on Kos, but it isn't easy."

We continued along, and presently she caught one of our number stepping on a mosaic. "Hello!" she said. "Why don't you look where you are going? You should look down, not up."

This restrained us all awhile, but soon we were treading carelessly again. Lena had her troubles with us. There was an unpleasant young woman in our group who often found something to fuss about. Now in our progress we paused near an antique chest. "Can one sit on this thing?" the woman asked provocatively, "or is it forbidden?" "It's forbidden," Lena said, "but do sit." Whereupon the woman sat.

Some of the palace rooms had grandiose Fascist murals in them, which, like so many other works of that pretentious era, are now falling apart — the paint looks moldy in spots, and it is peeling, or the plaster is cracking. Nor do the murals seem to have been much good to start with — rather they were hack jobs, devoted to the Fascist ideology. In one room we saw murals of the bread-making process — the reaping of grain, the baking of dough, etc. — that sententiously glorified the dignity of labor. "They remind one of the *Dopolavoro* idea," Lena said simply. Another mural showed a peasant feast at a long table, looking rather like the Last Supper; and the figures in the middle, she told us, were those of di Vecchi and his wife. They looked incredibly egotistical there, in 1960, and one wondered if they hadn't in the 'thirties, too.

Lena called attention to the poor quality of the work, but with her usual understatement — "The wall paintings are not of the best," she said, which was putting it mildly. The palace had a lot of lush furniture in it, too. We paused in one room that contained, among other things, an ornate, pompous Venetian-glass chandelier. "Look at this," said Lena quietly. "Murano glass, Napoleon III furniture, and a mosaic on the floor from Kos. It's not in very good taste, is it?"

The Greek government, she told us, is planning soon to remove some of the murals and more atrocious fittings, but one wonders if that will happen. It must be tempting to leave things just as they are, as a commentary, or last word, on the Italian occupation — the Greeks must have been horribly galled in the 'thirties, with the Fascists strutting in the Dodecanese and talking of *Mare Nostrum*.

That afternoon many of the *Aigion*'s passengers took a bus-trip to Lindos, a port on Rhodes's southeast coast, but I went off on foot by myself, for a swim and a stroll through the town. Rhodes has a number of Turks still living in the medieval city, and I wanted to see them and their quarter — there were four or five mosques there, for one thing, whose domes and minarets enhanced the skyline. I found a couple of them open, but the others were locked and seemed disused. I walked in the quarter for some time, on cobbled streets between houses that had harem windows in them — little screened balconies where women could sit without their veils, but still in Islamic modesty, and peer at the street life.

That evening I wandered through the town on my own again — the boys being off on a party with some other passengers. I found two nice little cafés that were run by Turks — one belonged to a man named Moustapha, according to its sign, and the other to an Achmet. Both served good *souvlakia* — spitted meat chunks — good *ouzo* — which the Turks would call *rakö* — and good imported beer of several kinds — instead of the invariable *Fix* of the Cyclades and Athens (for the Dodecanese are allowed free trade, to soften their new membership in the Greek economy). Moustapha's café was especially pleasant, with tables in the open under a gnarled old plane tree, and with the cook standing there too, beside a smoky charcoal grill. The *souvlakia* were served with parsley and onion-shreds, and little heaps of salt. The cook-smoke billowed up into the plane tree — which in Asia would have been called a *chinar*, I suppose — and off to one side a musician played Greek or Turkish songs on the harmonium.

The next day, early, we called at Budrum. Under its old name, Halicarnassus, it had been one of the famous Greek cities of Asia Minor. The original Mausoleum — the tomb of the ruler Mausolus — had been there, and Lena led us to a height above the town and told us about it. The Mausoleum had been one of the Seven Wonders of the World, so she asked us — like children on a quiz program — what the others had been; and between us, with childish pride, we finally answered her. She also told us the story of Artemisia, who had been queen of Halicarnassus during the Persian wars.

"Artemisia, like all the Greeks of Asia Minor then, was a subject of Xerxes," Lena said, "and she personally commanded a ship on the Persian side of the battle of Salamis. But when the battle was going against the Persians, and Artemisia was hard pressed — according to Herodotus — she suddenly pretended to be on the Greek side, and rammed and sank another ship of Xerxes'. This induced the Greeks to leave her alone, and it also did her no harm with Xerxes himself, for he was watching from far off and couldn't see well. He thought he saw her ramming a Greek ship, and he turned and said to one of his lieutenants: 'Our men have behaved like women today, and our women like men.' "

Except for Lena's commentary, on this and other subjects, there was little to be learned there of the ancient city — for the remains have nearly all disappeared — and we soon broke up and descended to the modern town. We got some good Turkish tea there — black tea, sugared, in small glasses — and some of the passengers found a camel or two to photograph, but it was not a place that I enjoyed much. It seemed dead and run down after the Greek spots we had been visiting. There are wonderful things to see in Turkey, of course, but modern town and city life, in my experience, are not among them. What I got mainly at Budrum was a feeling that I had crossed the line sharply into Asia — from the West into the East. It is a feeling I have got often in Greece and its neighborhood — and got from the past there, too, as well as the present. The Trojan Wars were between Europe and Asia. So were the Persian Wars; and Herodotus, their spellbinding historian, has made the differences between Greeks and Asiatics seem enormous — indeed, the later West's discrimination against Asiatics seems to have been conditioned by him. Thanks to him, in no small part, a Westerner feels that he is going off an edge of some sort when he reaches Asia, and I had that feeling now, in Budrum. I wasn't courting it especially, and I was happy when a launch came and took me back to the *Aigion.*

Later that morning we stopped at Kos, which I had visited before and shall not dwell on. Then we got back on the ship and steamed toward Patmos. We had lunch aboard, and after it I spent much time on the boat-deck — sunbathing, dipping in the little pool there, and watching the brown Dodecanese float by. We made Patmos at tea-time, and shortly before that Lena gave us English-speakers a briefing in the bar; she explained that the island's monastery — and the Grotto of the Apocalypse there — were too small for our group to maneuver in, especially as all the other language groups, from the *Aigion, Kriti,* and *Semiramis,* would be there, too.

The *Kriti* and *Aigion* landed at much the same time, it turned out, with the *Semiramis* well behind us. The monastery of Patmos is on a hill, and a vast number of donkeys and small mules were waiting to take passengers up there. I walked up myself — part way on a secondary path — and as I went along I began to hear, in the offing, the whoops and yells of the muleteers and donkeymen, as they fell to urging on their now laden animals. "Yea!" they kept crying. "Yea! Yea!", and they shooshed and clucked and whistled in the distance.

Soon my path curved around and joined theirs, and they made a lively sight. Passengers in all kinds of brilliant plumage — red hats, blue shirts, yellow trousers — and sitting astride their little animals, were going upward in a steady stream along a narrow, cobbled road, with Patmian men and boys, switch in hand, egging them on. I joined the parade myself, and found that many riders were feeling silly on their mounts, over which they had scant control. Some of the bigger ones were feeling ashamed, too, at weighing down such tiny creatures. They joked about it self-consciously, though really they needn't have worried — the fattest men there weighed less than other loads I've seen put on Greek donkeys.

Finally, as fast as the switches could drive them, they reached the village at the top, where they dismounted amid hawkers selling souvenirs — including lace doilies in a fish shape, which are a Patmian specialty. The muleteers didn't

tarry there, however — not at all — for they saw the
Semiramis in the harbor down below. They seized the
bridles of their animals and hurried down the road again —
whooshing and shouting "Yea!", and brushing past the later
upcomers of our party. It all made an active, swirly scene,
much like a round-up.

The sights at Patmos *were* crowded that day, and I had
seen them before, so I shan't describe them now. Nor shall I
say much about Delos, to which we devoted the next morning. Lena was in top form at that famous sanctuary. She had
endeared herself to all of us by now. "One thing nice about
our guide," I heard an old lady say on Delos, "is that she
always finds a shady place to talk to us in." Another passenger, an Englishman, remarked on how quickly she got
around. "I think she's identical twins," he said, gazing at her
fondly. "I could have sworn she was back there a second
ago." And he pointed far to our rear.

Lena too was more familiar with us now, and jocular.
"There's a special tourist step," she said. "Have you noticed
it? The feet are very heavy." She walked a few paces, picking her feet up and putting them down again slowly. Meanwhile, between the pleasantries, she took us around au-
thoritatively and tactfully — saying "very probably," for
instance, when someone volunteered an absurd explanation
for something she had already made quite clear.

Her English was good, though not like a native's. She told
us how the ancient Athenians had "purified" Delos — how
they had removed all corpses from the island and decreed
that no one else should die or be born there. "All the
moribunds and all the pregnant women were transported to
Reneia," she said, pointing to the island just across the channel.

Ten flocks of tourists — from the three boats — landed
on Delos that day, but the site is so spacious that it wasn't

overcrowded. Later in the morning I left our party and
climbed the little Delian acropolis. Looking down, I saw
files of tourists moving among the ruins like columns of ants.
They weren't black, of course, like ant-columns, but multi-
colored, with blue predominating. In the heat and brightness
of those islands, blue is a favorite color with nearly everyone; you always see it there; and it is, not surprisingly, the
Greek national color as well — sky blue along with white.
I stood looking down awhile on the blue-specked ant bri-
gades, then I descended and rejoined Lena. She had come
to the end of her tour and was giving advice on how to
photograph the famous Delos lions — ancient statues lined
up, in a row, beside the sanctuary. "I think," she said, "that
one of the best places to take them is from under *that* lion"
— she pointed — "from between its legs. Then you can get
the others, too, and they will be framed by the first
one."

Our camera-wielders dispersed to try this, then in time we
all drifted back to the *Aigion*, and it set sail. We stopped
at Mykonos that afternoon. The boys jumped ship there, to
stay for a few more days, and I returned to Athens.

Other group cruises, varying in length from half a day up
to several, are available on the Aegean in summer, and one
may also take a Black Sea cruise from the Piraeus — I did
that myself in 1959, along with my third son, Peter. Our
boat, though Greek — the *Hermes* of the Potamianos Lines
— had begun its cruise from an Italian port, and it carried
French passengers almost exclusively, for the enterprise had
been booked in Paris. Only half a dozen of us boarded at the
Piraeus. We left there late one night, made the Dardanelles
the next afternoon, and went up through the Bosporus early
on the second morning, just as dawn came on. It is a lovely
waterway, and that was a lovely time to see it — with a

series of vague mosques, fortresses, and other mysterious buildings silhouetted on the shores.

In the Black Sea we stopped, as I remember it, at Odessa, Yalta, Sochi, Sokoumi, and Batum. Except for Odessa and Batum these are all watering places, so we had a chance to see Russians on holidays. They seemed poor for the most part, and they were jammed into big communal hostels belonging to labor unions and the like — one felt, on looking at these hostels, that bedding and personal effects were actually bulging from their windows. As buildings they were crude and pretentious, too, but the people we met in the streets were plain and friendly, and interested in America.

I didn't see any of the luxurious villas that are said to exist in the Crimea, but this was not because my movements were restricted. I was allowed to walk as far as I could in the day or half-day we spent in each port, and sometimes I took advantage of this. I walked through lovely farms and pine-clad hills behind Yalta, and in all the towns Peter and I walked the crowded esplanades a lot.

Of course we didn't learn much of substance about Russia in so brief a visit, but we did get a glimpse of it, and the trip helped to fill out our view of the old Greek spheres of cultural influence — the Black Sea was colonized by Greeks in ancient times, and Orthodox Christianity went up through there on its way to Russia.*

* Recently — in the nineteenth century — many Greek communities existed in the Black Sea ports. Mykoniats lived together in Rostov and other Russian cities rather as they now live in Joliet, Ill. They engaged in commerce and shipping. The Greeks are not strong around the Black Sea now, but traditionally that region is a part of their world. The Turkish Black Sea ports — Trebizond, etc. — have also been Greek through most of history, though their Greek populations left after the troubles of the 1920's.

Our fellow passengers were almost as strange and interesting, furthermore, as the natives ashore. I know little of French society — and my command of the language is too poor to pick up subtleties in that field — so I can't say what shades of the French community were with us. There were ten or twenty French-Armenians, for certain, who got off at Batum with the intent of traveling by rail through their old motherland and then back, again by rail, to West Europe. There were several enthusiastic leftists aboard, too, I gathered. But many of the passengers seemed to be well-off, respectable middle-class folk. Peter and I sat at a table with, among others, a wine-grower from near Bordeaux and his wife and sister-in-law; and from their conversation one wondered why they had ever left home. Those two ladies were *soignée* in their dress, and so were many other of the women passengers. We also had a fashion show in the course of the voyage, and charades that were staged with elaborate costumes brought along for the purpose.

The passengers were scornful, on the whole, of alien food — whether Greek or Russian — and the cruise had a special French steward and French chef along, to see that the Greek staff did nothing barbarous. I don't wholly understand the motives of French tourists in the Mediterranean — except, of course, for real intellectuals or people just wanting a nice cheap, sunny vacation. American tourists often have a motive of duty when visiting Greece — from childhood up the place stands for civilization, or education, to us; and when we finally get to it we are resolved on some good conscientious field-work. But the French don't seem to be that way, perhaps because their own civilization seems so perfect to them — at least these on the *Hermes* weren't. They seemed to look on the cruise, rather, as a new means of killing time. Anyway, we had a pleasant week or ten days

with them, and then peeled off at Istanbul, or Constantinople, on the return trip.*

Many tours, of course, treat Greece as an incident in a
larger schedule — even a round-the-world one — and I
sometimes, in my year there, crossed paths with these. One
striking example was the so-called International School of
America, a party of students who were circumnavigating
the globe, by plane, with a staff of four or five teachers to
instruct them at their stops — in each of which they stayed
for a week or two. Another example I ran into was a version
of Swan's Hellenic Cruises, which are run from England
and which cover various parts of the Mediterranean basin
under scholarly guidance. The one I met up with came
through Greece in September, and it was due to stop later at
Turkey, Cyprus, Lebanon, and Yugoslavia (with optional
side-trips, by air, to Syria and Jordan). It had as guides —
if that word is exalted enough — Sir Mortimer Wheeler, the
archaeologist; Sir Maurice Bowra, the classical scholar; Sir
John Wolfenden, also a classical scholar and the Vice-Chan-
cellor of Reading University; Sir Harry Luke, an expert on
Cyprus; Mr. Stuart Perowne, an expert on Palestine; and at
least two other experts on the past, namely Canon Guy
Pentreath and the Reverend Lawrence Waddy.

I had some friends on the cruise, whom I met in Athens,

* Istanbul was called Byzantium when founded as a Greek colony,
by the Megarians, about 657 B.C. It was called Constantinople after
Constantine made it his capital in A.D. 330. And now the Turks, who
entered in 1453, call it Istanbul, though that name too is basically
Greek — it comes from the phrase *stin polin*, meaning "into the city."
Greeks still like to say "Constantinople," but the Turks stand fast on
"Istanbul," and it is a bone of contention between the two peoples.
When among Greeks in Greece a Westerner is apt to say Constanti-
nople, and when among Turks — or when visiting the place — he will
normally say Istanbul.

and they told me about a full course of lectures given aboard by these scholars, not to mention a big supply of reading-matter dispensed; and I believe that this and other cruises of the same organization — it puts on four a year — are probably the best things of their kind available to the average man. I went down to meet this particular cruise at the Piraeus and then accompanied its passengers — in one of eleven buses — back to the Athenian Acropolis. The passengers were very British looking, and they were dressed in smart casual garb of all varieties — shorts, slacks, suits; shoes, sneakers, sandals; etc. Most of them had sweaters, for the day was cool, and I even saw a couple of shooting-sticks among them.

My bus was the last of the procession, and when I finally reached the Propylea, the entrance structure of the Acropolis, I found one scholar, Canon Guy Pentreath, just launching on a talk about it — about how, for instance, the structure had been hard to build because of the slope there, and how the architect had solved this by using both Doric and Ionic columns in the design (Ionic columns are tall and slender, relatively speaking, while Doric ones are short and thick).

The Canon finished; we went, as next directed, to the Parthenon's south side; and there we found Sir Mortimer Wheeler awaiting us on the steps. He was tall and thin, with curly gray hair, a gray moustache, a pipe, a brown pork-pie hat, a gray suit, and brown suède shoes. "A charming lady of our party," he began, "said to me on the boat: 'I suppose you love looking at ruins.' I answered: 'No, Madame, I *hate* looking at ruins, whether archaeological or human.'"

Sir Mortimer turned out to be a showy speaker, with a gift for theater. "The Parthenon can best be described as petrified intelligence," he said. "There is intelligence in every line of it." The Greek mind had been essentially mathematical, he continued, and the Parthenon had a wealth of mathematical subtleties in it, which gave it life. He mentioned a few of them — the columns leaning slightly inward; the corner columns being closer together than the others; and the pedestal — the steps on which he was standing — being convex — curving to a slight rise at the building's center.

"Of course the Parthenon is now only a broken frame," he continued, "from which the picture has all but disappeared." He mentioned the big statue of Athena that had once been in it, and the vanished reliefs — the frieze and metopes — that had adorned it. "Most of that frieze is in another place," he said delicately — he was referring, as everyone there knew, to the British Museum — "and it owes its preservation to that fact." He began talking about the reliefs — the so-called Elgin Marbles, which Lord Elgin removed from Athens around 1800. "When you go back," he said, "if you go to a certain museum you will see good things, and less good, in that frieze." He advised his hearers to discriminate. "As Hellenists we are apt to be snobs," he said flatteringly. "There is nothing wrong in that, and not all classical things are good."

Then he spoke disparagingly of another temple, the so-called Theseion, which one can see from the Acropolis — it had none of the Parthenon's virtues, in his opinion — and also of a very different building near it: the Stoa of Attalus, a restoration of an old market-building, done by American archaeologists a few years ago and used as a museum. "The Stoa was rebuilt by my old friend Homer Thompson," Sir Mortimer said. "He did a good job of it. But *why?* What was the use, with such a dull building?" * Sir Mortimer shrugged elaborately and made a face. He was an actor.

After he finished, the party broke up for a while and was shown details of the architecture — and shown statues in the Acropolis Museum — by a number of Greek guides who were on hand, partly, I gathered, because the law forbids tours within the country that are conducted wholly by foreigners. The day was cool and cloudy — unusual for Athens in September — and the wind blew up little, gritty sandstorms from time to time, while the guides, each with a small train of tourists, ranged thoroughly over the Acropolis's flat top.

One lady guide I overheard seemed to resent Sir Mortimer a little. I saw her pointing over the Acropolis escarpment. "That is the Theseion," she said, "which Sir Mortimer Wheeler doesn't seem to like, and that is the restoration of the Stoa of Attalus, which also doesn't seem to appeal to Sir Mortimer." She spoke in a dead-pan way, yet I felt she was making a subtle Greek reprisal against what she took as Northern condescension — also, of course, the subject of the Elgin Marbles is apt to get Greek backs up. But Greek humor was much more in evidence. "Mind your hats," I heard another lady guide say near the breezy parapet. "Please don't consecrate any of your hats to the Goddess Athena." And the tourists with her laughed.

After a while Sir Maurice Bowra took over, speaking about the Greek theater. He had planned to do so in the actual Theater of Dionysus, which the Acropolis looks down on, but it happened to be closed that day — because

---

* One reason why: countless old Greek temples remain to us, but there are few structures, apart from the Stoa, that show the setting of ancient business life (and see page 175).

of some labor trouble — and he gave his talk on the height instead. He was a stocky, ruddy, middle-aged, energetic-looking man, wearing a beige sweater and smoking cigarettes. He stood up on a boulder and gave a strong and authoritative-sounding talk. He spoke of the limited resources of the Greek playwrights — they had only four main actors to work with, for instance, and these all male — and he told how such disadvantages had been compensated for, to some degree, by masks, elaborate clothes, high heels, and other devices. "But everything really depended," he said, "on the gestures and the saying of the words." Then he spoke of the particular theater down below us. "This Theater of Dionysus was the father of all the others," he said. "It was much the most important theater in Greece." And he went into details of its construction. "That screen down there," he said, "was probably put up by Nero, when Nero himself performed." He said other things, too, but I had a date then in the city, and I had to leave.

VII

ATHENS

After September, when my children and visiting friends had left Greece — when the "season" was pretty much over — I settled down to enjoy Athens and examine it more closely. My flat had a terrace and was in the section called Ilissia, half an hour's walk from the city's heart. Like most of Athens, that section was undergoing change — with new apartment-houses shooting up between old mansions and old hovels — yet even so it was quiet. The Athenian air is calm in October. The sky is blue then and the colors bright, and in the outskirts you can hear a dog bark half a mile away. My terrace had all this tranquility, and it was a fine place for writing, reading, or just basking — it was paved in terrazzo with a marble surround, and it faced southeast, so it got the sun from early morning until tea-time.

It also looked right out at, and lay parallel with, Mount Hymettus, which is a great Athenian landmark. Besides getting honey from Hymettus, the ancients foretold the weather by observing the clouds above it, and they loved the sequence of pink and mauve tones it assumes in the late afternoon — in the hour when Socrates, according to Plato, drank his hemlock. The mountain is long and nearly hori-

zontal, and its silhouette took up most of my horizon — its
ridgeline being three or four miles away, through the crystal
air. It was made of nearly solid rock — limestone and marble
— with a light sprinkling of dirt and a coat of scrubby vegetation, on which the bees did their feeding; a plant that
looked like heather was blooming on the mountain in
October, and if I walked there I would find each clump of it
abuzz.

When I waked in the morning, Hymettus would be
green and sharp of outline, with the sun rising, in the blue
sky, from its northeast end. By noon the sun would be high
above the other end — shining on a host of dust particles to
make a haze through which the mountain would seem gray.
By mid-afternoon that phase would be over, with the sun
getting around on my side to make the mountain green
again; and finally that would also pass, toward sunset, and
the rose tones would begin — Hymettus was long, spare,
simple, uninhabited, and nearly unforested, yet is was always fun to watch.

It was fun to walk on, too, and many Athenians did that
of a Sunday. They gathered mysterious herbs and flowers
there — with the Greek love of nature and what grows in
it. One Sunday evening in October I came down the mountain homeward bound, at dusk. The city lights below me
had been coming on — white streetlights and, in certain
sections, many-colored neons. The city itself was dark, and
getting darker by the minute, yet the Aegean — off to my
left beyond the Piraeus — was still blue. In the gloom, as
I descended, I saw a woman bending over a live-oak thicket
picking acorns. She looked old and heavy, and she had a sack
with her. I walked on, in the gathering blackness, and soon
a man overtook me on the path. He too looked old, but thin
and genteel. He had a beret and musette bag, and was strid-

ing down the slope with flowers in his hand. He walked on, and I lost him in the nightfall — I had all I could do to grope my own way home then.

On weekdays I would walk not on the mountain but into the city, going there for dinner, or for a late lunch, if I could bear to leave my terrace. The streets would be sunny then, and my way would lead through residential districts, some of them quite new — proceeding up a rise and then dropping to the region of Constitution Square.

I would do one or two errands there — cash a check, say, or buy a book — then have lunch in a *taverna;* and afterwards I might walk around and see things. I might visit the Acropolis, which I could reach by walking through the Plaka, the oldest part of town. Athens is a big city, and it was far from small in ancient times, but in between it shrank. After the triumph of Christianity it was frowned on as a holdout of paganism — in A.D. 529 the Byzantine Emperor Justinian closed down the Athenian philosophy schools, which had persisted until then. Later the city dwindled to a provincial town, being less important than other Greek centers in the Byzantine era — much less important than Salonika, for instance, in the north. Under the Turks, who entered in 1465, it declined still further, and it was little more than a village in the eighteenth century, when West Europeans began visiting it again, and sketching and describing it.

Its revival dates from 1834, when it was made the new nation's capital, and began its furious modern growth. Despite its great age it now often seems more like an American city than a European one, because it is so lacking in the impediments to growth — like walls, old houses, and narrow twisting streets — of a real medieval town. To the extent that such things exist in Athens they exist mainly in the Plaka, which lies under the Acropolis — to its northeast — and has always been inhabited, apparently, since classical times. The oldest still-extant buildings in the Plaka — little stone-and-plaster houses left from the Turkish period — are on the lower skirts of the Acropolis itself — on the slopes of detritus that fall away from the cliffs. They can be reached by steps and narrow alleys, and they are much like the stone houses on some Greek islands. They are fun to wander among — the people in them don't seem to mind strangers, and the alleys are high enough to have a good view of the city.

Just below that part, where the Plaka starts leveling off, one finds houses built soon after Athens became the capital, when people were converging there from other liberated regions. These houses, by and large, are in a neo-classical style rather like that of the Greek Revival buildings in some cities of northeastern America. They are chaste and graceful; they are apt to be painted in subdued earth colors; and they use many details taken straight from ancient models — they often have "palmette" finial tiles along their eaves, for instance, like those on classical temples. Many old Athenian houses look not at the street, but inward, onto courtyards and green gardens, where cats forever come and go. Such houses are being shouldered aside now, by apartment buildings and other modern structures, yet they still do dominate the Plaka, and they make it a lovely place for strolling in the autumn clarity.

From the Plaka one can look straight up at the Acropolis — one sees a rugged, overhanging gray-brown cliff with a masonry wall atop it. That part is much too steep to climb, and to get up one must go clear around to the other end — the western — where a winding flagstone path ascends to the Propylea, the sanctuary's entrance gate. The buildings on the Acropolis — the Propylea, Parthenon, Erechtheion, and Temple of Athena Nike — exceed most visitors' expectations at nearly any time, but on fall afternoons they are at their best. The marble they are made of, from Mount Pentelicon, was nearly white when quarried in the Periclean era, but it has taken on a brownish-yellow, golden, creamy tone with age. It has a trace of iron in it that slowly oxidizes to make the change. Pericles and his architects knew nothing of this, presumably — they must have thought their temples, except where painted, would stay white — yet they could hardly complain now if they saw them. The stones with eastern exposure, on the whole, have weathered the most. In patches — vague ones, thanks to the subtleties of wind, sun, and the marble itself — the Parthenon's east end has turned almost the color of butterscotch. Elsewhere the building is paler, and in some places, where the action has been slow, it has scarcely departed from its native snowy (or vanilla ice-cream) color. But all in all its tone is warm, and the golden autumn sunshine brings this out. The autumn stillness surrounds the Acropolis, too — a plateau high above the city — and from it one looks at the neighboring mountains and looks far to sea. The sun in autumn sets out beyond the sea, and beyond the distant Peloponnesian mainland. It gleams off the water and makes the old stones blaze, then drops away in silence.

The other classical sites of Athens — they are relatively minor — can be seen from the Acropolis and can be visited from it on foot. The city's museums are farther flung, on the whole, though one of them is on the Acropolis itself and another is just below it, to the north. Athens is a good museum city, but that side of its life is not organized quite as New Yorkers, or even as West Europeans, might expect.

When one gets to the Eastern Mediterranean one finds, as a rule, that the contents of the museums get ever more interesting, and their housing ever more primitive. There is one great exception to this rule — the museum in the Jordan side of Jerusalem, which has a superb plant, financed by the Rockefellers, but relatively little in it because the inhabitants of Palestine have not gone in much for graven images. The rule is well exemplified, though, in Cairo, where the chief museum has a spectacular collection of statuary and of smaller things, like Tutankhamen's jewelry, all jammed together as in a warehouse. Athens comes between these extremes. The Greeks have little money to spend, so they must do without the latest tricks of lighting and showcase design, yet they also have an intelligence, and an appreciation of their past, that helps them make a little go very far.

The city's principal museum, the National Museum of Archaeology, is devoted wholly to ancient things, chosen and arranged on artistic, or art-historical, lines (as opposed, say, to social-historical ones). It has especially outstanding collections of painted pottery, of ancient Mycenean treasures, and above all of sculpture — of sculpture in all the technical categories of "archaic" (down into the fifth century B.C.), "classical" (fifth and fourth centuries), "Hellenistic" (third, second, and first) and "Roman" (from then till the start of Byzantine times, in A.D. 323). Innumerable statues were carved in Greece all through these periods — through the well-known cycle of the primitive, the ripe, and the decadent — and many of the best have been collected in the National Museum. They are still being collected, too, as excavations proceed; and the National — despite the tons of Greek statues carted off to Europe in the past — is undoubtedly the world's leading museum of ancient Western art.

The Acropolis Museum, which is on that eminence itself, is similar in emphasis to the National, but more limited in material — it is a small establishment, devoted to things found right on the site. It too has much fine sculpture, mainly "archaic" and "classical" — it has the best collection, outside the British Museum, of reliefs from the Acropolis temples.

Besides these two, Athens has in the Stoa of Attalus — which stands beside the ancient Agora, or city market-place, at the foot of the Acropolis's north slope — an antiquities museum with a different bias. The Agora has been excavated in the past few decades by American archaeologists — under the banner of the American School of Classical Studies — and a museum in the Stoa now displays the best of what they have found. As the Agora was the center of old Athenian business and politics, and as many people lived in and around it too, the museum has a mine of evidence on how the old Athenians managed their affairs: how they cooked, drank, and kept their persons, and also how they voted, adhered to standard weights and measures, and even ostracized the fellow Athenians they thought too popular (there is a sizable collection in the Stoa of *ostraka*, the pottery chips on which citizens wrote the names of those they would ostracize, and in some cases these show signs of mass-production — an equivalent, perhaps, to ballot-box stuffing).

Aside from its ancient collections — pre-Christian almost entirely — Athens has two leading museums, the Byzantine and the Benaki, devoted to later periods. The Byzantine — housed surprisingly, but charmingly, in a Florentine-style villa — has a wealth of icons, carvings, fabrics, and church jewelry that help, along with Athens's many old churches, to make the city a center of Byzantine study — the equal, in that regard, of Ravenna, Mount Athos, Salonika, or Constantinople. The Benaki Museum, named for a rich Greek family that created it, has many fine Byzantine items too, plus a big collection of more secular medieval and modern *objets d'art* and handicraft things. It is a good general museum of post-classical Greek works.

Tourists are surprised, sometimes, to find that Athens has no museum of painting. Plans are afoot to establish one, but the question of what will go into it is a puzzle. The ancient Greeks made paintings — as good as their statues, to judge from what the ancient writers said — but little remains of these except for murals and what was done on pottery. Greek Byzantine painting, again, is interesting in the extreme, but it is so religious that it calls for separate display. Of pre-modern Greek secular painters, only El Greco has left much of note, and there is some question whether he shouldn't be called generally Mediterranean — or even Italian or Spanish — rather than Greek. Then finally Greek modern painting, however good, is hardly more than an offshoot of French painting — it has never developed initiative of its own. Instead of the Renaissance the Greeks got the Turks, and this rather put them out of the European movement. It is an oddity of their cultural history that gets expressed — along with other aspects of the same thing — in the Athenian museum set-up.

Museums, archaeology, and the tourist business all seek, in their ways, to explore the past and convey it to modern humans. This activity is going strong in Greece now, and the style in which it is conducted has local peculiarities, thanks to history and other factors.

Archaeology in Greece is close to the humanities, for one thing. In North America and the Pacific it is close to the social sciences, especially anthropology. The archaeologists there, like the anthropologists, are exploring primitive folk-ways. If such archaeologists visit Greece, for one reason or another, they find themselves in a strange world where their colleagues seem mainly interested in the aesthetic quality of sculpture or in tracking down some literary reference — this bias gives archaeology in Greece, some think, an ivory-tower quality.

Then the tendencies of the different nations who have been digging in Greece have made themselves felt. In the nineteenth century, when archaeology was becoming a rage in the Christian world, Greece was a weak, newly liberated country that had to let her big neighbors dig her soil up for her. The French, the British, the Germans, and the Americans did this, among others. The French dug up two of the greatest classical sanctuaries, at Delos and Delphi — both sacred to Apollo — and in exploring the material there, and describing it, they indulged a bias toward the spiritual and aesthetic side that may have reinforced the ivory-tower quality mentioned above. The Germans dug up Olympia and many other places, and in *their* handling of the material they indulged a pedantry that sometimes discolored it — the light Greek touch in art and letters does not lend itself to solemn analysis, though it has gotten much of that in the past hundred years. The British and Americans didn't color their results so much, perhaps — they concentrated on producing them and did so in considerable volume. There is a modern British specialty in archaeology — very strict *partial* digging up of sites, by trenches or pits, with the remainder left scrupulously intact around these, for later digging or merely for showing the stratigraphy (the relationship of the ancient layers of occupation). This method has had great success in the Middle East and in Roman Britain itself, but it hasn't caught on in Greece, where some archaeologists, at least, believe in peeling whole layers off their sites — and where the clues from stratigraphy are reinforced, also, by those from the ancient writers. Literary sources are vital to classical archaeology in Greece, and the good archaeologist there is a well-read man. Some important Middle Eastern sites, on the other hand, have no literature at all to go with them.

Greek archaeologists themselves are taking over more and more now, as the twentieth century unfolds — foreign ways of doing things may count less in their country, in the future, than Greek ones. Even an expert, perhaps, would have a hard time defining the emergent Greek style in archaeology, but there are a couple of things that can be said about it. For one thing, Greece is still a poor country and cannot lavish vast sums on excavations any more than it can on museums — her archaeologists must choose their sites carefully; read the ancient writers a lot; dig in a small way; and keep a lookout for the chance finds that come with road-building and other non-scholarly earth movement.

Secondly, Greek archaeologists are better fitted than foreign ones to study their own ancient literature — ancient Greek differs a lot from the modern, but it is taught rigorously in the Greek schools, and Greeks are gifted linguists anyway. It seems likely, therefore, that archaeology in Greece will continue and enhance its literary bias as time goes on; that its marriage with the humanities will prosper; and that this will make itself felt increasingly in the museums and the tourist life. Tourists who linger on in Greece, going to museums and contemplating the past, may find themselves still more involved with considerations of art and poetry.

I didn't go deep into such things in my fall in Athens — I only sensed them vaguely from the outside. Actually I was doing many other things besides museum-going, one being a continued pursuit of the Greek countryside, with which I was still infatuated. On most of the Sundays in October and early November I walked over Mount Hymettus to the Mesoghia, the "Center of the Earth," the rich farming plain that lies between there and the sea — I had already come to know it a little in the spring. I walked up to a pass in Hymettus's northern end, which took two hours from my flat, and then down the other side, which took one hour till I reached the first Mesoghian town. As I looked down from the pass, the Mesoghia was a big expanse of earth — now tawny, now reddish-brown — sometimes running flat for miles, sometimes billowing up into hills. There was a verdant sheen on the plain from its vineyards — their grapes just harvested, in September — and the place was spotted, too, with olive orchards. Here and there dark cypresses grew beside some little church, and here and there some village had pines and fruit trees near it. But there were no forests — the plain had been cleared and cultivated for three or four thousand years, at least. It ran eastward, from Hymettus, for ten miles or so, then curled up into some rolling hills, beyond which lay the blue Aegean. Northward, to my left, the sea faded off to the big island of Euboea, which was a hazy olive green in those days. But out ahead it merely lay there drowsily — blue in the warm sun, beneath white clouds.

I would gaze at this view awhile, then descend the mountain and walk on the plain, stopping for lunch at one of the towns there — they all still seemed ancient, but at the same time bustling, prosperous, and full of vitality. I would order

specialties of the region — *retsina* and charcoal-broiled lamb
chops, together with bread and a salad of some sort — and
these would come in large quantity, and fine quality, at a
cost much lower than in Athens. After lunch I would continue walking till the early dusk, when I would end up at
another town and catch a bus back to the city.

The weather all this time was gorgeous for my purpose
— warm and sunny — and I would feel hot and burned in
the noontimes. But by November it began getting bad for
the farmers, who expected the rains to begin and who complained of drought. The dust grew thick in the Mesoghia.
It lay like red-brown flour on the fields and cart-tracks. It
went down a few inches, and below that the ground was
hard, so the farmers couldn't plow. I didn't see how they
could have planted, either, at least to much effect — I didn't
see how the seeds could have sprouted in that dryness. The
olives didn't develop right, either, somehow; they are supposed to be harvested in the fall — shaken off — and they
need some rain, it seems, to make them leave the trees easily.
These problems were apparent as I walked on the thirsty
plain, and I began hearing about them too — even in Athens
everyone was talking of them. I heard also that the drought
on the islands was severe — that on some the peasants were
slaughtering their young stock for lack of grass. And I
heard often that people were praying for rain.

The rains did begin late in November — weeks behind
time, but copious once they started, so the farmers soon
caught up. After that we often had clear days, but the fall
was not the same again — we didn't recapture the endless
old still, sunny magic. I also broke my routine about then
with a small program of traveling. I had seen almost nothing
of North Greece, and I wished to make a couple of trips
there before the year was out. I embarked on the first of

them — a bus-jaunt to the Pindus mountains, in Greece's
northwest — at the end of November in company with a
friend named Raoul Cohen-Faure, a writer (he was bent on
extended travels, it so happened, and I planned merely to
accompany him for the first few days).

We left Athens early on a Tuesday morning, having reserved front seats in a bus bound for Trikkala, a town on
the plain of Thessaly, a hundred and fifty miles to the north.
We drove out first through Boeotia, a province that borders
on Attica — Athens's own province — to the north and
west, and that was often at war with it in classical times.
The heavy rains had been on for only a few days, yet we
could see the results already. We drove through rolling
hilly country, and the earth there was now colored different
shades of chocolate. Most of the land was rocky — not
arable — but there were small fields here and there. Some
were being plowed as we drove by, and in others the bright-
green wheat was already showing.

We passed through Thebes, the Boeotian capital — the
scene of the Oedipus legend — then traveled along a big
plain named Copias, which is fertile anyway, being arti-
ficially irrigated — a reclaimed lake. The poplars and aspens
by the road there were turning yellow, and yellow leaves
lay on the wet ground.

We went on, and soon began climbing into hills. They
were wild and craggy — the hills that make the historical
barrier between North Greece and the Athens region —
the pass of Thermopylae, where Leonidas held the Persians,
is at their eastern end, where they join the coast.

We didn't go near Thermopylae, but several miles inland
from it. The road climbed up between airy crags, and
looked down on deep valleys. There was gnarled limestone
all around us, with jags everywhere, and peaks like trun-

cated cones. There was green grass in the valleys, and oak trees, changing color, on the slopes. We went on through this country, twisting and turning, then came to some cliffs and made our way down them to a flat plain.

At noon we reached a town there, Lamia, and stopped awhile — Raoul and I had lunch in a *taverna*. Afterwards we went through more mountains — smaller ones — and got into the plain of Thessaly itself. It is the main breadbasket of Greece, and it is huge by the standards of that country — it stretches away dead flat interminably. It was green and moist then, with farmers plowing on it and shepherds grazing sheep. We drove along a straight black asphalt road, with the blue sky reflected in it.

We got to Trikkala, our bus's terminal, around three in the afternoon, then changed to another, more local bus, to travel for an additional half hour. We were headed for a town called Kalambaka on the plain's northwest edge, where a pass comes down onto it from the Pindus. The town has some famous old monasteries behind it, which are set on pinnacles and are called the Meteora, or "Airy Places," and we planned to visit them.

We had the pinnacles in view all the way from Trikkala. They were made of limestone and weirdly shaped (like other limestone pinnacles I have seen in South China, around Kweilin, and in the Baie d'Along of Indochina). They were a blue-gray in the moist afternoon light, they stood up high and mysterious, and they had deep clefts between them. We drove straight at them, trying to puzzle out their formation, but not succeeding well.

Kalambaka, a little provincial town — or village, even — lay at their feet. The pinnacles rose straight behind it, and their tops, when we reached the place, looked almost like clouds above us. We couldn't tell much about their layout

from below — nor much about the monasteries on them —
so we shouldered our baggage at once and set out to climb
them (it was latish in the afternoon now, but a near-full
moon was due). We took a still more local bus around to
the pinnacles' side, then began walking up between them
— intermittently on paths and on an asphalt road — according to directions we got from shepherds and others along
the way. There were several pinnacles, it turned out, standing free from a bluff behind them and looking rather like
stalagmites. We climbed up, along rocky paths, and soon
began glimpsing the monasteries, of which five or six are
now in existence, though there used to be many more —
each was on a pinnacle of its own, like the mushroom castles
that one used to see in fairy-tale illustrations. A few centuries ago (we learned the next morning) all the monasteries
had used this isolation for defense against bandits. They had
been approachable only by ladders, or drawbridges, or
ropes hauled up on winches, all of which could retreat in
times of danger, to make the sites well-nigh impregnable —
and also, of course, to add to their monastic seclusion, for
each had been, in theory, like a colony of pillar-saints.
Those days were ended now — there were permanent
bridges leading out to the pinnacles, and permanent, if
tenuous-looking, stairways carved upward in the rock —
sometimes showing on the face, and sometimes disappearing
into tunnels. The monasteries seemed run down and nearly
deserted, too, and the new asphalt road that served them —
plainly for the benefit of tourists — detracted from their
mystery.

We reached the bluff-top that lay behind the pinnacles
and walked along it, examining the monasteries in the twilight. We were heading for one of them, the farthest, which
we had heard had a hostel for visitors, but as we drew

near it a monk came out and shouted, across the intervening
chasm, that the place was closed for the season. So we
turned and walked back down to Kalambaka in the moonlight.

We found a little hotel there, had dinner and a good
night's sleep, and the next day attacked the pinnacles again.
The monasteries themselves, we found, were not too interesting — they were demoralized, with only a handful of
beggarly monks in them; and their icons, though sometimes
good, seemed less so than many elsewhere in Greece. Actually the monasteries gave one a bad feeling, of institutions
petered out and turned to parasitism. But as landscape they
were well worth seeing — the closest realization on earth,
perhaps, of the mushroom-castle dream.

Kalambaka was pleasant, too. It had a true mountain feeling — cold mud and damp air in the streets at night — cold
winds coming down from the heights. While walking back
to it that first evening we picked up fine village scents —
of corn roasting, pine wood burning, and all the animal
smells — of cows, horses, donkeys, and their stables. The
bus station, where we spent some time, was in a region
on the edge of town that was dominated by old tires, coffee
shops, mud, primitiveness, and general dirt. It reminded
me, nostalgically, of bus-station precincts on the edges of
Chinese and Indian towns. Such places seem all to be the
same, essentially, and one imagines that they are descended
straight from the caravanserai life that prevailed until a few
decades ago.

That afternoon we got into another bus — we had the
front seat again — and started up through the mountains.
We were traveling on a dirt road now, and heading for
what I believe is the highest road-pass in Greece, atop the
main Pindus ridge. That is the divide that separates eastern

Greece from western. It is the country where the Greeks stopped the Italians in the Second World War — the Italians were more numerous and better armed, but the Greeks stopped them in the Pindus and threw them back into Albania.

As we went up the first valley, the afternoon sun shone brilliantly on a forest of plane trees there, which were turning, almost like maples. The trees were golden and the grass around was green. We kept on going, up and up, as sunset came, then darkness. We passed lonely stone villages beside the soft brown road. We rose higher and higher, and it got colder, but before we reached the pass itself we entered a cloud — or a fog, as it seemed. The driver kept stopping, and an assistant of his — a boy — kept getting out to wipe the windshield. He would also adjust the carburetor for the altitude, and adjust the lights to get under the fog. We groped our way along. There were some chickens in the bus's rear, and they clucked, and the peasant passengers shouted commonplaces to each other. We puttered along this way, crossing the pass at some point, then finally descended from the cloud and saw bright lights far below us, to the left. They came from Metsovo, a mountain town where we would spend the night.

We had an introduction to a hostel there, which was part of a museum run by the Tositsa Foundation, a philanthropy of the family with which Evangelos Averoff-Tositsa, the Greek Foreign Minister, was connected. The museum's caretaker met our bus and took us there, and the place was like an oasis in those chilly heights. The museum was designed to show the old life of the region, and the hostel was furnished accordingly. Our room had natural pine paneling, unvarnished, and heavy pewter-colored hardware. On the walls hung bright carpets — tapestries, more strictly, for traditional Greek rugs have no pile — with the colors red, green, and black predominating. There was a semi-circular white-plastered fireplace — with a rug, again, hung around its mantel — and also a narrow upright stove, which the caretaker now stoked with pine chunks and made hot. We went out for dinner in the town — noting, among other things, that cordwood was stacked high in the streets — then we came back and had a snug, warm sleep.

The next morning we gazed out the window at a ragged mountain landscape, with light-green fields below dark pine-woods on the facing slope. Beneath us the town fell away, and what we looked down on were rough slate roofs on the houses, and rough stone walks between them, giving an over-all gray, and grainy, and rugged effect.

We had breakfast in our room, then the caretaker led us off to the museum. It was a reconstruction of an old Tositsa house, baronial in style, from the centuries before the Greco-Turkish war of the 1820's. It was a small fortress, largely self-contained, and I guessed it was like many es-tablishments of the lower Balkans in the Turkish period — we were in Greece politically, of course, but geographically we seemed more to be in the Balkan wilds — we seemed worlds away from Athens and the Aegean. The house's ground flood had a stable in it, with thick stone walls and little barred windows. That story had a ceiled courtyard, too, with a running fountain; also store-rooms with oil and wine casks; and arms and saddlery. On the floor above were kitchens and other store-rooms capable, our guide said, of holding a November-to-April food supply for the whole house. A good deal of this supply was stocked now re-alistically — cheese, garlic, herbs, and grain in bins. Shelves held heaps of oregano and of an herb the Greeks call moun-tain tea, which they boil and drink. Elsewhere the house had a big sewing-room, where the women could comb wool, and spin and weave and make the family clothes. There was much handsome wood-carving in the place, which is typical of mountain Greece — there were wooden bins, churns, water-tanks, chests, cabinets, and balustrades, all nicely worked — and wooden ceilings with molding patterns in relief.

There was fine brass and copper-work too, and signs of Turkish influence in this and the other crafts. The bedrooms had low tables, at which one could sit on the floor in the Asiatic style. They had broad sleeping platforms, with rug-covered cushions ranged around their edges. Two reception rooms had big rugs on the floors — in reds, blacks, blues, and greens, with touches of yellow and orange. And these and other rooms had museum displays of old Greek mountain costumes — of *evzone* skirts, long stockings, pompon shoes, and so forth.

Later that morning we were shown Foundation works elsewhere in Metsovo, including schools, a hospital, a lumber mill, and especially a dairying and cheese-making enterprise. The Foundation was out to raise the standard of living in those mountains, and it had imported Jersey and Brown Swiss cattle, which it was crossbreeding and interbreeding with the local varieties — sending good calves out to chosen families for foundation stock. It was also trying to replace the sheep's-milk cheeses of the region with more sophisticated cow's-milk ones — it had built a cheese factory for this purpose and had sent two youths to Italy for training. These things were all explained to us — as the Foundation's director showed us around — in Italian, which Raoul knew well. They spoke a lot of Italian in that western part of Greece.

Meanwhile, and later, we looked round Metsovo. The

scenery there was Alpine, with snowy peaks in the distance, against the blue sky. Before lunch we walked out to one edge of the town, along a slope. The air was clear there, and we saw a crooked, silver river far below us. A cold wind blew behind us, and all around were straight pines with their shadows. We heard mule-bells approaching; and far in the distance, on the slopes there, we saw a trail winding off into the mountains.

That afternoon we left Metsovo, again by bus and again in the front seat, en route to Iannina, the capital of that whole mountain region, which is called the Epirus. We had a baby on the bus this time, in a cradle, and again we had peasants shouting amiably. We drove through further mountains and through two valleys. In the latter we saw Vlach shepherds, wild mountain tribesmen, with their flocks and great big dogs — they come down to those lowlands every winter, we were told, from the heights off toward Albania.

We drove on, and just before dusk we descended on Iannina itself, a misty walled town beside a lake — we stayed there a couple of nights and then parted, I flying back to Athens and Raoul continuing by bus to the Greek west coast. On the morning of our day there we went out to Dodona, a nearby classical site — an old shrine of Zeus with a famous oracle, which had expressed itself through the rustling of oak leaves. The sanctuary was in a big valley, with a high bare mountain to its west. There were ruins of a temple there, and of a Byzantine basilica, and of a classical theater that had been excavated and partly restored. There still were oak trees, too, standing noncommittally now, with their leaves half-gone in the autumn.

We walked in Iannina a lot. It had been Turkish up to 1913, and it still had much Turkish architecture in it, including two mosques — one of them now a museum —

overlooking the city wall. The lake was big, and calm as a mirror; it had an island on it, with monasteries, and it was said to contain many carp and perch, as well as eels. I took in much of this, but my thoughts were turning to Athens, and I didn't mind leaving the next morning. I had a good flight down, the first half of it along the Pindus mountains' western edge. From the plane I looked on wild, steep hillsides closely terraced. I looked from above on the razor edge of cliffs, and into deep gorges, with streams there on their gravel bottoms. The sky was wet and ragged on that morning, and there was lots of green now in the mountains.

Back in Athens it was winter. We still got sunny days, and they were clearer than ever, with the dust washed from the sky by rain. But in between we had big storms. I could spot them in advance by watching Hymettus — much as the ancients used to do, I suppose. The main clear-weather wind of Athens — it is related to the *meltemi*, and blows all summer and much of the fall — is from the north. Then as winter comes the blow is more and more from the southeast. The wind comes from the Aegean — from the Cyclades — all laden with rain. It blows against Sounion, the southeast point of Attica, then comes across the land to the Mesoghia and to Hymettus. From Hymettus's northwest side — my side and the city's — the change is first seen as clouds peeping over the ridge. They may be small and white, especially in the early fall, then as the storms grow serious they get darker and bigger. When the winter is really on they loom and lower there, and they move fast, northward. When the clouds are racing on Hymettus you can expect no settled clarity — it is only when that wind dies down, and a sure one from the north sets in — after some uncertainty — that you can count on sun.

The rain rains hard at times. From my terrace I could watch it hit a nearby apartment-house, blowing up from the south. It would hit the tall side of the building all at once, in a gust, and then the water would bounce and crash down like a waterfall. My terrace wasn't much fun in that weather, but the top of Hymettus could be fun if I went up there. If I stood in the pass the mountainsides would come and go in the mist, like something sensed vaguely in a Chinese painting.

Athenian life was deep indoors now. The passing tourists were long gone — with a few exceptions — though that didn't mean that all foreigners were gone, for there is a year-round population of Western expatriates in Athens. Lovers of the past — and haters of modernity — are drawn to Greece. So are the sexually unorthodox, for the place has always been tolerant of that. So are beatniks, miscellaneous escapists, and quite a few serious writers and painters. So are do-gooders, archaeologists, and sensitive people of means who merely like the atmosphere. The Athenian foreign colony is numbered in the thousands. Some of its members are precious — annoyingly cultist about unspoiled Greek islands — but others make stimulating company. The colony is divided into many subsections, which have their own relations with each other and with the Greeks — on the borderline they intermarry a lot with the latter and blur with them almost wholly, for the Greek people are among the most cosmopolitan on earth, welcoming strangers and going abroad in droves to live among them.

Greek foreign relations on the personal scale are ramified beyond description. It would take a whole book to write about the Greek-Americans alone, and there are lots of them in Athens now — not the old, poor first-generation ones so much (if these return to Greece, they are apt to go to their native villages), but the young, Americanized second-generation ones, who are on hand — with their knowledge of American ways and the Greek language — to serve as middlemen in the present close relationship of our countries. These second-generation Greeks have been through the fierce American melting-pot, which insists that its products forsake their ancient culture. So while many of them appreciate Greece, others are apt to be down on various of its customs — on the dowry system, the close family ties, the ways of the Orthodox priesthood — even, perhaps, on the *retsina* and the olive-oil cooking. Not for them the cult of unspoiled islands — but the complaint, rather, that Athens has no television. They can make a better living in Athens at the moment than they could in Providence or Chicago, but they miss the Coca-Cola, nonetheless. Their presence adds still more spice to the old-world capital (and there are other spices in it, too numerous to mention — the bitter return, for instance, of so many Alexandrian Greeks, repelled by Egypt's nationalism).

The winter entertainments offered by Athens, with a few exceptions, are not unique — mostly they are theaters, movies, concerts, art exhibits, night clubs, and the like on Western lines — and sometimes of only provincial Western quality. One great exception is the eating and drinking in *tavernas*, and another is the so-called *bouzouki* music — a modern form coming right from the people, much as our jazz has done, or the Calypso and Latin dances of the Caribbean. The origins of *bouzouki* music are not clear. Some say it came over from Turkey when the Greek diaspora returned from there in the 1920's. Others say it grew up entirely in Athens and the Piraeus. Its sound is no clue to this riddle, so far as I can tell — it sounds both Greek and Asiatic — and probably would in any case. Its name comes from its leading instrument, the *bouzouki*, which is like a mandolin with an extra-brilliant tone — because, I have been told, of sympathetic strings. A *bouzouki* ensemble has two or more of these *bouzoukia* plus some other stringed instruments — a piano is often included — and perhaps an accordion and a set of drums. The players sit in a row or in tiers and play with a serious mien, like the jazz masters at Eddie Condon's in New York. Usually one bouzoukist is a sort of soloist and improvises cadenzas while the others follow — the art is wide open to improvisation, in both words and music, and it carries a lot of current folklore with it.*

Bouzouki joints are spotted here and there in the Athenian suburbs — several are on Phaleron Bay down near the Piraeus. They run very late at night — or in the early morning, rather, and they are brilliant in sound, appearance, and everything else — even in broken glass, for in many of them the customers may throw tumblers around if they will foot the bill. A big place will have a special *bouzouki* singer

---

* It is "neo-folkloric," I have been told by an Athenian musicologist. He says neo-folkloric music is common now in many parts of the globe — Asia, Africa, South America, etc. — being born of the action of Western music — brought by the radio and phonograph — on native styles. *Bouzouki* music has both native Greek and Western elements in it, he explains, plus the Turkish; the word *bouzouki* is Turkish, he has informed me, and so is the instrument. *Bouzouki* artists, like other neo-folkloric minstrels — Leadbelly is an example — often dwell on themes of crime and prison life. The composer Manolis Hadjidakis uses the *bouzouki* style, but raises it to an unusual degree of artistry, in the opinion of experts — Hadjidakis is esteemed in Greece for his highbrow, as well as his popular, works. His music for the film *Never on Sunday* is still being sung around the world now. It is also sung and played in remote corners of the Greek mountains and islands, where it functions almost interchangeably — at dances, etc. — with the old folk music.

or two — a man, say, and a sexy girl — and there is also much dancing by the clientele, solo and otherwise, on traditional Greek lines. The whole business is very Greek, very gay, and altogether enjoyable, and I took in some of that, too, as the winter set in.

Otherwise I was quiet, feeling the hibernation urge. I went through most of December that way, and for Christmas I withdrew to Kifissia, planning to embark from there on my second northern trip — to the north*east* this time — without wholly returning to the city. The Christmas part was very pleasant. I stayed in the Cecil, my old home — being cared for by the servants whom I liked so — and I walked in the community and called on friends. I stayed through Christmas and through Boxing Day, and on the morning of the twenty-seventh I departed — in the pitch dark, before seven o'clock — in dripping drizzly weather.

I left from the Larissa Station in Athens's northern outskirts. The day had lightened somewhat by the time our train — a short, fast diesel *automotrice* — pulled out. We went through suburbs paved with slimy mud — past innumerable of the little white houses, all helter-skelter, that Greeks are building around their capital. Mud paths lay between them, gleaming dully under the gray sky.

We reached the countryside, the northern Athenian plain, and there passed fig trees gray and bare again — and the grapevines, too, again were stumps. The mountains by the plain — Pentelicon and Parnis — were wrapped in clouds.

We went on northward, and the landscape was fog-bound for much of the day — visible for only a mile or so — though sometimes greasy clouds were lifting, or mists were running up and down a hillside. Wet flocks of sheep stood near the track, and wet shepherds in their winter

hooded capes. The plain of Thessaly was soggy, and green
with the new wheat — the sky was gray and dark, but the
ground was the brightest green imaginable.

We passed through mountains after that, and through the
wild and cragbound Vale of Tempe — like a magnified
Japanese garden — which is a famous sight of Greece. Later
we broke out and were in open country again — watching
the stone railway stations fly by, and watching the sodden
huts and sheepfolds. The human and animal worlds looked
miserable that day, but the vegetable one looked joyous —
half submerged, but brighter and fresher than ever.

We reached Salonika in mid-afternoon. It was still rain-
ing, and I went to a hotel there, planning to lie over a day
and see the city — it is the second largest in Greece, the
capital of Macedonia and the north. In the morning the
weather cleared — Salonika has a famous harbor, and its
water was calm then, and bright blue, with snowy mountains behind it. There are two Salonikas, really — a new
city on the harborside and an older, Turkish one on the
heights above it. The new part is laid out carefully, with
tall buildings, broad streets, and monumental vistas, while
the old has cobbled alleys wandering up its hillside, penned
in by Turkish-style houses — these built as usual with lots
of wood, and balconies, and irregularities (the house where
Kemal Ataturk was born — a few decades before the Turks
lost the city in 1912 — is in that section; it is painted a
deep red, a mulberry or salamander color). Salonika, like
Athens, is having a building boom, and new apartment-
houses of eight or ten stories are slashing into the old
Turkish part. The city has many Byzantine churches, too,
and I visited some of them, but the day was so pleasant that
I spent more time in walking.

At first the sun was pale and wintry, but by midday it was almost hot — I had lunch outside a *taverna* on the water-front, and it was delightful. Salonika is a famous place for eating. Its specialty is mussels fried in batter, but it also goes in for other meat and seafood dishes. Its *tavernas* lean more to red wine, almost, than to the white *retsina* of Attica and the islands (their open red wine, served in carafes, is excellent, and they don't seem to let it get vinegary).

The morning after Salonika I pushed on, again by train, for Alexandroupolis, a so-called city named after Alexander the Great, which is the last real town in Greece — in the panhandle of far northeastern Thrace — before you reach Turkey on the way to Istanbul. Greek friends had not encouraged me about Alexandroupolis, or what I would find there, but I wanted to see it anyway, and have a look at Thrace, to round my year out.

We set off early in the morning again, and the day was gray, though not too rainy. We started norward and then turned east, running not far from the Yugoslav, and later the Bulgarian, frontier. There were lakes up in that country, and also mountains, of course, and fresh green fields and poplars. We went under snowy heights that lost themselves in the clouds, and we saw dark bare fruit trees in the fields.

I was in an *automotrice* again — a swift, de luxe means of travel theoretically, though the non-de-luxe qualities of Thrace had altered this (apparently few rich Greeks go on that line unless they have to). I was in a first-class section, having bought a ticket for it out of curiosity. I think I held the only such ticket on the train, yet still the section, which had twenty-four seats, was full much of the time. People swarmed into it at the stations, and the management had long despaired, apparently, of stopping them —

weathered old peasants would sit next to me, gazing through
unaccustomed glass at their countryside, which was raw,
and crude, and mountainous, and bosky.

Much of the time we went along narrow valleys, with the
gray clouds pressing down on them. Brown rivers surged
along beside us. I had been reading of Thrace in Herodotus
and Thucydides. In the Persian wars Xerxes, according to
Herodotus, had taken his huge, motley Afro-Asian army
through there — they often drank the rivers dry, he said —
and I could almost feel their morale sinking in those mountains. Then in the Peloponnesian War — according to Thucydides — the Athenians and Spartans had fought interminably over the Greek colonies in Thrace; it had seemed
a dismal, distant contest as he described it — like a struggle
now for Patagonia — and as I gazed I could see why. Later
Alexander the Great, of course, had used Thrace, along
with Macedonia, as a base in his mighty effort to unify the
West and East; what I felt about *that*, as we rolled along,
was that if he could tame Thrace he could have tamed almost anything.

We went on into afternoon, and the dead-gray sky persisted. Sometimes there were green cabbages in the fields,
and always there were brown and wintry hillsides. Many
Turks are left in Thrace — they were exempted from the
exchange-of-populations agreement of the early 'twenties —
and now we saw signs of them from time to time. In one
town, Xanthi, we saw half a dozen mosques, with their
white pointed minarets. It was easy to feel that we were
leaving Christendom.

In the afternoon — the ride took all the daytime — I
was approached by a furtive, portly Greek. He had trouble
talking with me, for he knew no foreign language, and my
own Greek was badly limited, but he had something he

wanted desperately to say. He kept drawing sketches to explain himself, but he hid them cagily if he thought someone was looking. It turned out, finally, that he had old coins to sell — which was against the law, according to him — and he said he would bring them to my hotel in the morning, for he, too, was bound for Alexandroupolis, and lived there. He helped me find the hotel, indeed, when we arrived — it was a clean little place, and warm enough, but primitive.

The town was primitive, too. Good food it seemed to have — good seafood especially, for it was on the north shore of the Aegean — yet wander as I might I saw nothing in the shops but garish things — as if to dazzle the backwoodsmen — that must have come from Athens or Salonika. Alexandroupolis seemed to produce nothing itself unless one counted vitality. The people in the streets looked rugged and unrefined, and the whole place seemed typical of a frontier outpost, which it was. The Greeks seemed to be emphasizing it as that, in fact — as a punctuation mark at their country's end — for they had endowed the town with a little airfield, and snappy harbor installations, and nobler public buildings than seemed really warranted.

I glimpsed these things a little — walking, for instance, on the grand and lonely esplanade — but I didn't delve into them. Toward noon I went back and received the hot-coin merchant. He mysteriously unveiled two coins with the head of Philip of Macedon — looking like an Indian in a war-bonnet — and a few more of Alexander himself, but I did no buying. I looked at the wares respectfully, then changed the subject. Later I wandered some more in Alexander's City. Then I caught a small plane out of it, and that was the end of my year's investigations.

The earliest known high civilization in Greece was the Minoan, on Crete, which flourished in the second millennium B.C. and ended around 1400. It was succeeded by the Mycenean, which fell around 1150, yielding to a dark age.

Classical Greek civilization emerged a few centuries later. By the sixth century B.C. Greek arts and letters were in full swing, especially in Ionia (Greek Asia and the east Aegean islands) — Sappho and Pythagoras were among the early lights there. The expanding Persian empire encroached on that Ionian side of the Greek world, though; the Athenians led the other Greeks in aiding resistance; and finally the Persians resolved to cross into Europe and punish Athens. Their first expedition was stopped at Marathon in 490 B.C.; their second was stopped at Salamis in 480 and conclusively wiped out at Plataea in 479; and after that Europe was safe.

Athens had led the Greeks, essentially, in these wars, and afterward she led them in the arts of peace through much of the fifth century. It was in that century that Pericles governed, Socrates taught, the great tragedies were written, and the Parthenon, Erechtheion, Propylea, and Temple of Athena Nike were built on the Athenian Acropolis. In 431, however, Athens got embroiled with Sparta in the Great Peloponnesian War, which lasted till 404 and left her exhausted. Long, ruinous struggles followed between the various Greek states — Athens, Sparta, Thebes, Corinth, Arcadia, Boeotia, Euboea, Argos, Elis, Thessaly, Macedonia, etc. — till their unification by Philip and Alexander of Macedon in the latter part of the fourth century.

Alexander spread Greek rule to Asia and Africa, but on his death (323 B.C.) his Hellenistic Empire fell apart into warring states. The growing power of Rome was soon felt in that struggle; she destroyed Corinth in 146 B.C. and for centuries afterward was mistress in the Greek region.

Meanwhile Christianity appeared, began superseding paganism, and in 323 A.D. was embraced by Constantine, who made Constantinople the capital of his Eastern Roman or Byzantine Empire. This empire was Roman at first, but became Greek in language and outlook — the Orthodox faith was its religion. It lasted eleven centuries, though its rule was checkered — Arabs, Crusaders, and others held parts of Greece for long periods of its life.

In 1453 Constantinople fell to the Turks, who controlled Greece till 1821, again with local exceptions.

In 1821 the Greek War of Liberation began. It took long to complete — the Turks still held much of modern Greece in 1912. The new Greek government, dating from 1832, has been European in outlook and style — generally a monarchy. Greece fought a disastrous war with Turkey in 1919–23, followed by an exchange of populations. In the Second World War she went through a harsh occupation by the Italians and Germans. Then came two Communist insurrections, the second ending in 1949. They have been followed by an era of co-operation with NATO and the West — especially with the U.S., which became heavily involved in Greek affairs by the Truman Doctrine of 1947.

INDEX OF PLACES MENTIONED